"If you've hit a speed bump in your career, this guide will smooth out your ride and get you moving again. Darcy Eikenberg's strategies, at once eminently practical and deeply insightful, will help you see your work—and even yourself—in new ways."

DANIEL H. PINK, *New York Times*-bestselling author of *When, Drive,* and *To Sell Is Human*

"If you know that something has to change at work, but you aren't sure where to start, this is the book for you. It's a practical and fun guide that will help you take control of your professional life without compromising what matters most."

DORIE CLARK, author of *Reinventing You* and executive education professor, Duke University Fuqua School of Business

"Darcy Eikenberg showcases a no-nonsense approach to escaping the noise in our heads and reclaiming our power. Her universal insights guide readers through difficult subjects like self-worth, doubt, and career planning with ease. *Red Cape Rescue* is a must-read for professionals of any age facing a fork in their career path. Let Coach Darcy hand you your red cape."

APRIL STERCULA, CEO, Baxter Marine Group

"I've spent countless hours helping friends and clients think through their career, but never felt like I was efficient in my approach. Until now. Darcy Eikenberg gives us hope paired with process, a foolproof way to supersize your work, your life, and your impact on the world."

"For anyone who's tired of being stuck, this book is like Goo Gone for your career—no matter where you work. Smart, actionable, BS-free, and totally on the money."

"Coach Darcy's book can turn even the most miserable, anxiety-provoking work situations—including the infamous 'I'm stuck and don't have the energy to figure it out'—into an action plan that will excite you, a team, or a whole company. With a fun and pragmatic approach, she will nurture your inner cheerleader and knows just the right words to say for forward progress, even when it's all still imperfect."

"A smart and engaging book by a professional development master. Darcy reminds us that productivity and happiness need never be trade-offs for career success."

"Darcy provides practical strategies and techniques to help you take back control of your career on your own terms. *Red Cape Rescue* will reset how you think, revise what you say, and reinvent what you do."

MATTHEW TEMPLE, senior director of alumni career and professional development, Kellogg School of Management, Northwestern University

"If you're at a crossroads, looking for actionable advice, or just want great perspective, Darcy's words are game-changing. For over five years, Darcy has coached me through some incredibly tough and important career decisions and has always helped me see my strengths in new ways. She will do the same for you. Grounded in real-life examples, this book is a reminder of our own power and will give you the confidence you need to move forward."

AMANDA FERBER, managing director, 22squared

"Inspiring, thought-provoking, and stirring right from the start! This captivating book on mindset reminds us how we are able to cast our own vision for our life. When we listen to the nudges, express gratitude, and learn from our mistakes, we are able to move from surviving this thing called life to thriving."

CHRISTIN COLLINS, author of *Her Phoenix Rising* and global wellness thought leader

"If your work life feels like Groundhog Day, *Red Cape Rescue* can help. This book will give you guidance, through inspiring success stories and small action items, to change the parts of your job that no longer work for you."

COLLEEN SARINGER, PhD, first vice president,
lead wellness consultant, Alliant Insurance Services

"Rethinking your career? This book is for you. It asks the right questions to help you explore and find what's best for you."

PETE FRIEDES, former CEO, Hewitt Associates,
and co-founder, Managing People Better

"*Red Cape Rescue* is a must-read and so relevant in today's challenging work environment. I highly recommend this book as it will give you practical tips to apply today so you can soar in your career and life."

LISA O'NEIL, system director,
marketing and brand management, Lee Health

"This terrific book takes the mystery out of career transitions and reads like a super helpful conversation with a knowledgeable and experienced career expert. We can be happy at work. Author Darcy Eikenberg shows us how to make that happen with humor, inspiration, and practical steps."

JENNIFER B. KAHNWEILER, PhD,
author of *The Introverted Leader* and
Creating Introvert-Friendly Workplaces

RED CAPE
RESCUE

SAVE YOUR CAREER
WITHOUT LEAVING YOUR JOB

Sandra,
Time to soar

RED
CAPE
RESCUE

DARCY EIKENBERG

Darcy

●● **PAGE TWO**

Cataloguing in publication information is available from Library and Archives Canada.
ISBN 978-1-77458-164-3 (paperback)
ISBN 978-1-77458-165-0 (ebook)

Page Two
pagetwo.com

Edited by Kendra Ward
Cover design by Kelly Small and Fiona Lee
Interior design by Fiona Lee

RedCapeRescue.com

To Mom,
who soars through it all.

CONTENTS

WHY YOU AND
YOUR CAREER DESERVE
A RED CAPE RESCUE

M Y CAREER rescue began in a cold McDonald's parking lot.

Earlier that day, I'd left my Atlanta office in a typical rush, hustling to catch a plane for the February leadership meeting at my consulting firm's headquarters in suburban Chicago. On my way out the door, my assistant shouted that I'd just missed a call from my boss, Suzanne, who wanted to talk before the next day's gathering.

Since I'd see Suzanne in person in about eighteen hours, I was concerned. Never one to create unnecessary drama, she'd told my assistant that nothing was wrong and to "call when you can."

Now, in those pre-iPhone, pre-Bluetooth days, "call when you can" meant using two hands to dial your shoe-sized flip phone—practically impossible when navigating I-75 traffic or hauling carry-ons through airport lines.

Not surprisingly, with me on the move and Suzanne booked in meetings, we kept missing each other.

Finally, as I white-knuckled my rental car down the icy highway toward my hotel, the phone rang. It was now past eight at night and I didn't want to miss her again. I steered off the road, parked under the safety of the Golden Arches, and answered the phone.

I could never have guessed what would happen next.

Greetings from the future you

But before I tell you more about my past, let's talk about your present.

My guess is you've picked up this book today because you've hit a speedbump, setback, hiccup, or hitch in your once reasonably fine career.

That shift might have originated from the outside, sparked by huge changes touching the whole world: an economic crash, contagious illness, environmental tragedy, or government uncertainty. Or your career chaos might have been ignited by changes only visible to your company or profession, such as:

- a technology breakthrough replacing what you know or sell
- an explosion of offshore, outsourced talent
- the consolidation of a big customer or competitor
- a merger, acquisition, or spin-off
- or a leadership shake-up involving your C-suite leader, your boss's boss, or maybe your direct boss

Alternatively, the "shift" might be hitting the fan quietly in the confines of your own marvelous mind, heart, and soul. Maybe you've been motivated by a health scare affecting your body or that of someone you love. Or you've missed one too many of your children's concerts or competitions. Or perhaps you're counting the birthday candles on this year's cake and asking one enormous question: "What do I do *now*?"

If my guess is right, you're wishing for a hero to save the day.

Perfect. You're in the right place.

Meet your new hero

Without further ado, let me introduce you to the super-human talent who'll make the most difference in your successful long-term life at work.

That person is *you*.

Yes, you. Right where you are, just as you are.

Oh, wait—were you thinking it was *me* who'd liberate your life at work?

Nope. I'm not your hero.

I'm here as your humble guide—Coach Darcy at your service. I am not your rescuer. But as a credentialed coach, mentor, and teacher to accomplished corporate professionals all over the world, I do have one powerful lifeline to throw you: the strategies within this book.

Applied together, they'll help you create what I call a Red Cape Rescue. That's where you can save your career and succeed on your own terms at work. What's more, I'll show you how to do this without the default, drastic interventions of finding a new job, starting a business, bowing to an early and unwanted retirement, or, worse, compromising your health and happiness, along with that of those who love you.

It's a big promise, I know. But here's what else I know. Through our work at RedCapeRevolution.com, people all over the world are using these techniques to take back control of their professional lives with clarity, confidence, and courage. My clients, audiences, and readers have discovered how to reclaim their own lives at work and create positive, surprising changes in their career experiences, often right where they are, just as they are, without settling or sacrifice.

You'll meet many of these folks along the way in this book (with names changed to protect their privacy):

- They're part of a new movement that shouts *no!* to wasted weeks, months, or years spent frustrated or feeling stuck. They abandon the conventional wisdom that says, "Be happy you have a job."

- They've learned that at the first flashes of frustration or discontent, they don't need to reflexively hunt for a new employer, launch a new business, or just give up and stop striving.

- They're practicing ways to rethink what's possible, even in the most structured corporate environments, knowing they have more power to take back control

What if you could change your life at work without having to change everything in your life?

than they ever thought possible, and more ability to make an impact than they ever imagined.

These brave souls changed their lives at work without changing everything in their lives. I want that for you, too. I want you to be the hero of your work life and charge forward toward your own career rescue.

But first, you'll need an important accessory.

Every hero needs a red cape

Remember when you were a kid and you'd grab a towel or a sheet and fling it around your neck? You tossed your shoulders back and stuck your chin out. You felt confident; courageous, even. And, most importantly, you felt your life was in control as you stood there in your imagined red cape—even if you only controlled the backyard.

Now, fast-forward to your world of work, where life right now may feel anything but in control. What if you could step into a hypothetical phone booth and emerge with your red cape on, layering you with new strengths and confidence? What if you could have that superpowered feeling in your professional life, anytime you wish, no matter what is happening around you?

I believe you can. In fact, I believe you must.

I'm handing you the hero's guide

Every rescue organization, from your nation's emergency services to your local firefighting unit, has a guide, a playbook, a day-to-day reference. At its simplest, this guide is a list of strategies and techniques that all new recruits must master and every veteran must remember each time they're called into action. With its contents honed by deep experience and painful mistakes, the guide offers proven tools and decision-making frameworks these heroes can learn today and use as they respond to specific crises tomorrow.

In this book, I'm handing you the guide I've developed over the years as a successful coach of leaders and high-performing professionals battling all kinds of career and personal change. I'll teach you the simple, practical adjustments you can adapt to your own career situations, right where you are now, just as you are:

- In Part I: Reset How You Think, you'll learn how to shift your mindset and build your confidence, getting clear on what you control and what you don't.

- In Part II: Revise What You Say, you'll gain fresh strategies for more powerful conversations with your colleagues, and even with yourself.

- Finally, in Part III: Reinvent What You Do, you'll discover how to battle the blocks, protect your time, and move your career forward.

In addition to offering you these superpowered concepts, this book also contains actions to put in motion right now—ideas that work in the real world, tested by real people just like you. You'll find these steps in the Action Plan sections at the end of each chapter. To make it even easier, every Action Plan is in our free toolkit at RedCapeRescue.com. There, you'll also find checklists, scripts, videos, and other resources to put these ideas into action and get relief even faster.

The techniques here will help you rescue yourself inside your own career. Some of these strategies might resonate with you more than others. That's okay. My suggestion, though, is that you learn all of them now, since once you learn them, they're yours for life. After all, the Boston ladderman may never fight a raging brush fire in the forest, but if one day he finds himself in Bozeman, he'll have the skills to adapt.

Now back to the parking lot

As I sat inside that chilled rental car, flip phone pressed to my ear, I listened as my boss, Suzanne, told me she'd decided to retire and had already chosen her successor.

It wasn't me.

When I hung up, I expected to feel like a day-old McNugget: cold, rubbery, and stale. After all, Suzanne's role was the next step up the traditional corporate ladder for me. It was the job I was expected to want, the one others assumed would be my logical goal.

Instead, a realization hit me: I was . . . relieved.

I'd never wanted that job. I searched my soul for a tinge of sour grapes, but suddenly I knew it'd always been true. That job would have meant moving north permanently and experiencing more freezing nights like this one, spending more time on politics than people, and working even more hours than I already did.

But if I didn't want that job—and let's face it, I wasn't getting that job—what *did* I want?

I wanted a Red Cape Rescue for my career. Of course, I didn't call it that at the time, but in hindsight, that subzero night was a catalyst for all that happened next. I didn't want to settle. I wanted to soar.

Today, I'm grateful to Suzanne, and to the question "what do I do *now*?" because everything since has brought me here to you.

The world needs you

Although I'm here to serve as your faithful champion and I want to see you standing confident once again, I'm also mindful of the bigger stakes at hand. I mean, our world is filled with problems. Okay, your company might refer to them in code, calling them "challenges" or "opportunities." But no matter what pretty name you give it, you know much is broken.

But then, there's *you*.

You with your unique superpowers: that mix of strengths, skills, resources, and talents you bring to work each day. You with your special abilities to influence and choose and help.

Knowing you're out there, I feel hope.

By picking up this book, you've already launched your Red Cape Rescue. Together, let's regain the clarity, confidence, and courage you want and need to thrive in your career, on your terms.

Let's help you take back control, to become the hero you're proud of in your work and your life. We need *you* in our world of work, now more than ever.

It's time to soar.

PART I

RESET HOW YOU THINK

We do not need magic to transform our world.
We carry all the power we need inside ourselves already;
we have the power to imagine better.

J.K. ROWLING

Right now, you might feel overwhelmed, confused, or even angry about what's happening at work. I get it. But breathe—in this first step of our adventure, you'll unlock the secret to taking charge once more.

1

KNOW YOUR CORE POWERS

HERE'S WHAT I already know about you. You're smart. You're a professional. You're good at what you do. You don't like being stuck, unsure of your options. If you weren't all these things, you'd never see the need to think differently about your career in the first place. You're here because it's time to control the outcomes of your work and your life.

Truth is, everyone wants more control, more power over their own destiny. We *crave* it, even if we find that hard to admit sometimes.

When we don't have it, we generate what psychologist David McClelland calls "power stress."[1] That's the tendency to get angry and frustrated when others don't behave the way you want them to or situations don't play out as you wish. It happens to all of us, not only those of us who've labeled ourselves "control freaks" (you know who you are, my friends).

As part of the human race, you naturally hunger for more power and control over your destiny. It's in your DNA. In fact, I'm guessing the reason you chose this book is that you're ready to accelerate control over whatever's happening in your world of work.

Good for you. Let's get to it.

A list of everything you control

Ready? Here is the complete, conclusive list of everything in the world you control:

1   Everything you think.
2   Everything you say.
3   Everything you do.

Wait—that's it?
Yep, that's it.
So, that means everything else—from #4 to #4,000,000,000—falls outside your control.
That can't be true, Darcy. We humans now have incredible technology at our fingertips. We know how to manipulate the human genome. We can get virtually anything we want delivered to our homes within days or hours. We send humans into space for months at a time—and bring them back! Surely, we can control most everything, right? Right!?
Wrong. Here are a few things that fall on the "things you don't control" list:

- whether or not you get the promotion
- what your boss thinks of you
- whether the product sells
- whether you've helped or hurt
- whether the stain comes out
- how your colleague reacts
- if the client likes it
- whether the plane takes off on time

- if the recruiter thinks you're a good fit
- whether your email gets opened
- what the stock market will do
- how your mom feels
- and more...

Yes, you can influence a lot of these items. Throughout this book, I'll offer you specific tools to do just that. But to have complete and utter power over them? Not. Gonna. Happen.

Your Red Cape Rescue starts when you realize where your unique power lies: in what you think, say, and do. That's all. But don't fret, smart one. It's enough.

Myths and lies

Maybe you don't believe me. After all, growing up, you were likely taught you could do anything, have anything, be anything... if you only worked hard enough and did the "right" things. So you squeezed and stressed and tightened your grip around what you thought you could control until your fists hurt. As TV's Dr. Phil would say, how's that workin' out for ya?

Of course, your parents and teachers didn't mean to be wrong. They were trying to protect you the best they knew. There's a good reason why they believed what they did, and it's all about how our brains function.

We'll dig into this deeper in chapter 2, but here's an important fact (one we'll keep returning to): the human

There's a big advantage to knowing where your power lies: life gets easier.

brain is biologically programmed to try to keep us safe. In his book *Linchpin*, author Seth Godin notes, "Everyone has a little voice inside their head that's angry and afraid. That voice is the resistance—your lizard brain—and it wants you to be average (and safe)."[2]

Our internal desires for control are merely a well-trained response—an attempt to stay safe. But here's the rub: "safe" isn't a route to more meaning, impact, or happiness. It's only a route to more of the same. Or, as author John A. Shedd writes, "A ship in harbor is safe, but that is not what ships are built for."[3]

The good news here is that once you see what you control—and what you don't—you'll create a stronger sense of power, safety, self-worth, and freedom than you've ever had before.

How Blaine changed her mind about control

After years working at a major university, my client Blaine accepted what appeared to be an exciting new job at one of the world's leading tech innovators. *Finally*, she thought, *the career I've been waiting for.*

She got off to a fast start, connecting with colleagues, diving into the business, and even making a few new friends along the way. About four months into her new job, though, the company announced a restructuring. Blaine's department would now be led by someone new, and she'd be partnering with other folks in the company whom she didn't yet know.

The problems started early.

Initially, Blaine kept her head down, working on her projects as she'd been doing all along. Over time, though, she started to hear criticism. Questions. Thinly veiled judgments she interpreted to mean that she wasn't performing up to expectations. Nothing was said overtly, but she noticed she was being left out of meetings and calls. Even a few of the folks she had considered friends seemed... distant.

And in true human form, she began to worry, waking up at night and tossing the situation around over and over. She was doing the exact same thing she'd been doing before the leadership changes, so what wasn't working now? She tried to figure it all out on her own, but no solutions popped up.

Blaine didn't want to leave this job, nor did she want to lose it. She also didn't want to fall into the old-school, this-or-that thinking that she'd seen trap so many of her peers. She didn't want to choose between (1) diving into an exhausting, soul-sucking job search, abandoning all the good that existed where she was, or the alternative, (2) sucking it up and settling for a not-so-great work experience.

Her career was ready for option three: a Red Cape Rescue. Together, we identified actions that were clearly within her power and under her control, including what she thought, said, and did.

What she thought	When she caught herself thinking, *Something must be wrong with me*, she changed that thought to *I'll do my best to find out what's happening and fix what I can.*
What she said	One by one, Blaine scheduled conversations with her new boss and colleagues, as well as friends she'd worked with before the changes. Without judgment or anger, she told them what she'd noticed about their interactions and comments, and that she was concerned. She swallowed her pride enough to ask what they were seeing in her behavior that she might be missing.
What she did	After hearing specific feedback that she was appearing "cold" or "blunt"— behaviors she had intended as efficient and focused—Blaine could make specific changes. She now entered each meeting more self-aware, taking more time to interact and ask questions, and making sure to not rush the conversation when others needed a little more time.

After taking control, Blaine not only opened the door to better conversations with her colleagues, she also slept better, worried less, and overall felt more positive about her life at work.

Knowing what you control—and what you don't—is liberating.

The greatest advantage of all

There's one more advantage to knowing—and practicing—where your true power lies, day in and day out. Life gets easier:

- You'll approach the inevitable challenges more calmly, without that white-knuckle death grip.

- You'll cut through the noise faster and quiet down those worrisome "what if?" thoughts.

- You'll give yourself permission to let what you can't control go.

When I was struggling to learn this myself, a Buddhist friend shared this story: Imagine you pick up handful of sand. When you squeeze it hard, the sand escapes through your fingers. But when you hold it lightly, the sand stays in place.

So, my friend, loosen your hold. All will be well.

You now have permission to stop beating yourself up for what's out of your control—and to focus *only* on the things you think, say, and do. When you do, you'll reclaim your power and start recreating your life at work in a way that works for you.

ACTION PLAN: RESET HOW YOU THINK

Ready to dig deeper? Dive into these questions. If you're not sure yet of the answers, that's okay. There's no right or wrong in these exercises. Just give them a try, and you can always come back to them as you learn more about yourself and your career.

1. What's the biggest thing you're trying to control right now? Write it down:
   I'm trying to control...

2. Now, read what you wrote out loud. Is what you wrote *really* in your control—is it something you can think, say, or do?

3. If you can't control it, then break it down and answer these questions:

   - What can I choose to *think* differently about this issue?
   - What can I choose to *say* differently (or more frequently or more loudly) about this issue?
   - What can I choose to *do* about this issue?

———————

A supervillain hovers nearby, ready to derail your success (and maybe it already has). Let's meet this lowlife and vanquish it, for good.

———————

2

CONQUER THE BATTLE OF THE BRAIN

L ET'S TALK honestly about one of the biggest barriers you'll ever face.

No, it's not the economy. Nor is it your boss, your age, your weight, your credit score, or even your family. It is (drum roll, please) your brain. Yes, that tingly tangle of neurons dancing inside your skull and triggering everything you do in this lovely life. Your brain, pardon the expression, has a mind of its own.

When your world goes haywire and it's time to rescue your life at work, you can use your newfound power to control what you think. That means learning how to conquer the battle of the brain.

Wait ... where's the battle?

I'm sorry to tell you this terrible truth. Your brain isn't always on your side.

I mean, it does so many wonderful things, like remembering your favorite flavor of ice cream or the refrain of "Macarena" (good luck getting that out of your head now). But it's also constantly chattering at you, like a third grader on Cupcake Day, and its messages aren't always tasty.

Early Buddhist writings refer to this nonstop dialoguing as the "monkey brain," where thoughts swing from tree to mental tree. Those monkeys swing fast, too. In fact, University of Michigan professor Ethan Kross, author of *Chatter*, says we talk to ourselves internally at a rate equal to speaking four thousand words a minute out loud.

> To put this in perspective, consider that contemporary American presidents' State of the Union speeches normally run around six thousand words and last over an hour. Our brains pack nearly the same verbiage in a mere sixty seconds. This means if we're awake for sixteen hours on any given day, as most of us are, and our inner voice is active about half of that time, we can theoretically be treated to about 320 State of the Union addresses each day. The voice in your head is a very fast talker.[4]

Now, I've got no worldly idea how anyone could accurately measure the speed of our internal dialogue, but what Kross says rings true. In fact, here's a sample of my own thoughts from the last fifteen seconds:

Okay, let's get serious and finish this chapter... Maybe I should print out what I've written so far... Naw, just keep typing—butt in seat, doncha know... I'll set a timer and I won't leave my laptop until it rings... Oh, before I do that, I might need chocolate... Man, my kitchen needs cleaning... Let me just load the dishwasher and then I'll feel better... Damn! Out of dishwasher pods. Where's my grocery list? Do I have enough chocolate to get me through this chapter? My back hurts—why does my back hurt... Maybe I need to stretch. Or lie down... When can I stop writing and take a break?!

No wonder we're all exhausted.

What's worse: not all of our thoughts are harmless. Let's take another look at mine. (Gulp.) Unless I've taken control, my own monkey brain will easily drop some banana peels to slip me up, like these slimy suckers:

Okay, let's get serious and finish this chapter... LOSER! Maybe I should print out what I've written so far... BUT IT'S NOT ENOUGH SO DON'T BOTHER... Naw, just keep typing—butt in seat, doncha know... AND IT'S A BIG BUTT, TOO—WHEN ARE YOU GOING TO THE GYM? I'll set a timer and I won't leave my laptop until it rings... YES, 'CAUSE I'M A LOSER AND LAZY AND...

Ahem. You get the idea.

This painful and demeaning dialogue was brought to you courtesy of my brain. I hope it doesn't make you think less of me. Perhaps you see a smidge of yourself in there, too. That dialogue is the battle: the battle between what the brain says and what the truth is.

What my brain was telling me is not true. I'm not a loser. I'm not lazy. This chapter is almost finished and by some stroke of disciplined miracle, you're reading this book. #winner.

It helps to realize that my brain, yours, your mom's, the president's, your boss's—*all* work like this. But me and you and your mom and the president and your boss, we're not losers. We're not lazy. We're not any of the hurtful things our brains often tell us we are. With extreme apologies to Journey's rock anthem from the eighties, please stop believin'.

The brain, she means well—but she lies

Why? Why doesn't the brain paint us a path of lavender and rosewater, all easy and sweet smelling? It goes back to biology. So, let's meet our biological ancestor, Gorp.

Gorp lived in the Stone Age and happily sustained his Paleolithic family through a daily quest of hunting for game large and small. The archeologists tell us that Gorp's primitive brain was pretty tiny, both size- and content-wise. However, Gorp's gray matter did one thing really well: it sought out safety.

Yes, when Mr. Gorp heard a roar from a saber-toothed tiger with a taste for Gorpy meat, his tiny brain signaled him to stay inside and hide, remaining concealed and

Your inner dialogue is a battle: one between what your brain says and what the truth is.

safe. Gorp's brain—exquisitely equipped for the times—protected his physical safety, and so guaranteed the survival of his species.

Now, let's meet You, circa today.

Sweet, modern You has come a long way from the Gorp household (or cavehold, as it were). For one, you likely wear pants. However, we now know (thanks, modern science!) that your pants-wearing body still houses a remnant of Gorp's primitive thinking.

It's called the amygdala.

The amygdala, which in the old days would trigger us when we'd hear a tiger roar, now triggers us when we hear our project manager roar (even if she's significantly less likely to chomp down on our tasty flesh). The well-meaning amygdala works like an alarm to the body, alerting the hypothalamus, which signals the adrenal glands. Their job is to shoot you a dose of adrenaline, forcing your heart to race and blood to pump.[5]

And you thought your corporate structure was complicated, right?

Now, what do we do when we get that jolt of adrenaline? We might freeze and hide. Alternatively, we sweat, feel the flush in our face, and get defensive, with fists up and ready to protect. Emotionally (and sometimes physically), we're in fight mode.

Here's the truly wild thing: this ancient, reptilian physiological response no longer serves us in our modern context, where tigers are more apt to be seen on Netflix or our local zoo cam than in our backyard. Knowing this, it's your job to suit up and do a little compassionate combat if you want to win the battle of the brain.

How to override the safety switch

If we're biologically programmed to stay safe and protected, how do we allow ourselves to be bold and confident? How do we risk more to gain the greater rewards that we want, whether those rewards are time, freedom, happiness, money, or something else entirely?

To start, we've got to separate the voice of our lizard brain from the cooler, calmer voice of our true heroic self. After all, that lizard is not you. It's not your hero. In the long run, it's not even keeping you safe—it's keeping you land-locked when you should be flying high.

Author and Stanford professor Shirzad Chamine calls that voice a "saboteur." In his book *Positive Intelligence*, Chamine describes the various types of saboteurs and says all humans share one in common—"the Judge":

> The Judge is the master Saboteur, the one everyone suffers from. It compels you to constantly find faults with yourself, others, and your conditions and circumstances. It generates much of your anxiety, stress, anger, disappointment, shame, and guilt. Its self-justifying lie is that without it, you or others would turn into lazy and unambitious beings who would not achieve much. Its voice is therefore often mistaken as a tough-love voice of reason rather than the destructive Saboteur it actually is.[6]

In that snapshot of my monkey mind you read earlier, the Judge is the voice calling me *loser* and *lazy*.

Can you hear that voice inside your own skull? Good. It's time to learn to spot that freakin' faker and weaken its hold over you. How? Well, if you want to conquer the battle, you've got to learn how to spot the enemy. So, let's name it to claim it.

Yes, I'm suggesting you give that little annoying voice a name. Personify it. It doesn't matter what the name is, as long as it reflects someone or some idea in your life that's a bit irksome. For example, my client Aruz called her voice "Sister Anna," after a teacher who embarrassed her by chiding her constant talking. (Interestingly, Aruz now gets paid to speak all day, *thankyouverymuch*.) James named his voice "Lex," for Lex Luthor, Superman's nemesis. Erin, incisively, dubbed her voice "Li'l Trouble." See how that works?

A name makes it easier to separate your real, red cape–wearing self from that villainous, lizardy, safety-clinging brain. Use whatever moniker will motivate you for battle, whether that's the Joker or Darth Vader or Hannibal Lecter.

What to say when you talk back to your brain

Now that you've named the voice inside your head, listen for it. Practice teasing apart its exhausting and negative commentary from what's really true. Do this out loud, or on a piece of paper, like this:

When my lizard brain says...	I counter with the better thought that...
My career is out of control.	I can only control what I think, say, and do, so I'll focus on that.
There's so much to worry about.	Worry never wins. Let me focus my energy elsewhere.
Everything's broken right now.	Everything moves in phases; I know this situation will eventually work out.
I don't want to fail.	I never fail; I just learn and try again.
Everything I need to do is so hard.	I've done hard things before. I can handle this.
I'm stuck.	I can decide on the next small action, and trust that each action moves me forward.
I can't decide what to do next.	There's no wrong decision, so let me make one and learn from that.
I've got so much to do.	Everything that's important will eventually get done.
I'm smart; I should be able to figure out all this, but I'm struggling.	I'm smart; that's why I'm open to trying out the ideas in this book.
What's wrong with me?	Nothing's wrong with me. That's just my bratty brain talking back to me.

That annoying voice in your brain is not your hero. It's keeping you small.

This work takes practice, and it's rarely perfect. In fact, I practice every single day (and don't always succeed). But here's what I've learned: when you separate the fearful, judging thoughts from the real you—the heroic you—you regain energy and confidence, and you take back control over one of your biggest assets: your brain.

You're going to need it. So win the battle and actively, intentionally choose the thoughts that push you forward. Tell those voices that drag you down to go back to their cave.

ACTION PLAN: RESET HOW YOU THINK

Ready to conquer the battle of the brain? Get started here.

1. Pick a name for your lizardy, judgy, fearful brain. Have fun with this—pick an identity or avatar you'd love to tell to shut up!

2. Watch for situations where that voice shows up— perhaps even now, or as you continue reading this book. You might hear it saying things like:

   - "This kind of stuff works for other people, but not me."
   - "I've tried these things before, and they never work."
   - "My job's just a job; it'll never get better."

3. Using the voice of your inner hero, talk back. Depending on where you are and what works for you, feel free to speak out loud. This can be fun and powerful. Start with the ideas listed earlier in this chapter.

———————

When you're boldly pursuing what's next, don't underestimate the power of assets you already have naturally. Let's discover what you might have overlooked.

———————

3

UNVEIL YOUR VALUES

ONCE UPON a time, I worked for a gold-plated consulting firm. The firm was filled with talented people and provided a never-ending parade of interesting clients who had juicy problems to solve. I practically grew up in the place, moving from the "shut-up-and-tag-along" levels to, fifteen years and three cities later, earning partner and leader status and becoming someone to tag along with.

Yup, I looked like a lifer. Like I'd retire there, happily. But (not exactly spoiler alert), I wasn't happy.

Of course, I *looked* happy. I never complained in public, nor did I disengage from day-to-day client work or my leadership commitments. I built teams, sold projects, developed relationships, solved problems, and helped others get what they needed to feel successful.

Sure, priorities and pressures were shifting inside my company as we moved from a private boutique firm to a publicly traded entity. But as a partner, I'd benefited from those moves . . . hadn't I? Hadn't it meant more opportunity, a bigger playing field, more money, more growth?

Yes, and . . . those elements didn't seem to matter.

After that cold night in a McDonald's parking lot (the one I shared at the beginning of this book), I started getting honest with myself about what was working in my career, and what wasn't. I finally confessed to myself that something wasn't right, even if everything was looking good on paper.

But then I did what most people still mistakenly do. I followed the old-school, broken-thinking path that said all my problems would be solved if only I found the perfect new job. I fussed over my resumé. I worried, wondered, waited.

After many sleepless nights, cranky days, and intense interviews, I began getting offers to join other companies. Many required disrupting my life, whether that was moving to a new city or adding hours a week to my commute. Others had uncertain leadership, and although they said they valued what I could *do*, the jury was out on whether they would value *me*. Most importantly, I began to notice that those companies looked a lot like the one I was already in, and the roles I was being offered looked a lot like the one I already had.

Thankfully, each time I came close to saying yes to one of these offers, something stopped me stone-cold. I didn't have the language to describe it back then, but today I know that I was hearing the whispers from my future, more heroic self. (You'll learn how to hear yours in chapter 5.)

Yes, I came close to accepting the option of sucking it up and living with the discontent, as so many before me had done and too many still do. But when I calculated the years of career runway I still had ahead of me, I chose instead to start saving myself.

Every value is worthy on its own. (It's value-able, if you will.)

That's when I invested in my first professional career coach. My initial question to him: "What's wrong with me?"

I learned that nothing was wrong with me, and, surprisingly, nothing was wrong with my company, either.

We just held different values, and I never knew it.

Uncovering hidden values

You're a smart, sparkling person, and at least once in your life you've probably attended a cocktail party with other smart, sparkling people: ones who are both interesting and interested. Let's imagine that, at such a party, one of your new, caring friends asked this question: "What you do you value in your life?"

(Okay, maybe that's not normal party behavior. If, to get into the spirit of the thing, you have to imagine that you and your friend had gone for a couple of extra rounds at the bar, that's okay. The question still stands.)

If you're like most of us, you'd probably smile and dust off a few old standby answers about what you value:

- family
- health
- and maybe even happiness

Although these are noble values, I propose that they're not specific enough. A value on its own isn't a divining rod. You need to look at all your values combined to make the decisions that are right for you.

Case in point: actress Felicity Huffman long valued being a mother. In fact, she shot to fame as a beleaguered mom of four on TV's *Desperate Housewives*, eventually winning an Emmy award. After the show ended, Huffman translated her popularity into a blog on parenting, sharing her experiences of raising her two daughters, with all the challenges and imperfections that come with the territory of being a modern mom.

In 2019, Huffman was convicted in a broad-reaching college bribery scandal after paying $15,000 to have her daughter's SAT exam scores falsely improved so she could get accepted into her chosen schools. In a letter to the judge prior to sentencing, Huffman said, "In my desperation to be a good mother, I talked myself into believing that all I was doing was giving my daughter a fair shot."[7]

I'm not judging Huffman, nor doubting the idea that she valued being a good mom, and to her, that meant helping her children succeed. But what other values might have been at play here that led to her illegal actions? Security? Belonging? Not wanting her daughters to be left out? Each of us makes our decisions not just based on one single value, but on a whole set of values. These values become our internal operating system, a collective set of guidelines that drive our actions.

Hitting the piano keys

You've seen this conflict yourself, I bet, in situations like these:

- The friend who hits the gym because he values his health, but who won't schedule a colonoscopy. He might value safety more.

- The colleague who values freedom, but never takes a vacation. She may value accomplishment more.

- The online gurus who talk about kindness, but who also criticize public figures. They may internally value recognition, self-expression, or even dominance more.

This disconnect is a lot like hitting two neighboring keys on the piano. If you've ever put a keyboard in front of a two-year-old, you know how this sounds. Played one by one, each note is beautiful and perfect. But strike two side-by-side notes simultaneously? It's not harmony. It's just noise.

Author Mark Manson says it this way: "Most of us are incredibly adept at telling ourselves what we wish to be true, rather than what is true. But our values are demonstrated through our actions . . . The problem is that most people aren't aware this decision-making process is going on in our head."[8]

Our collective set of values drive us, whether consciously or subconsciously. As *Black Sheep* author Brant Menswar puts it, "A lot of values are important to you, but which ones are you unwilling to compromise on?"[9]

Your values are the soundtrack playing behind each scene in the movie of your life—but they're more than that, too. Whether you know it or not, they're running the show. So let's make sure you know exactly what those values are.

Decode your values

If it's time for something to change, then it's time to make your values crystal clear, right now. Let's unlock the vault and get those drivers down on paper, looking them over to see if they're a middle C or a B flat. Chances are, your values are a huge clue to what's out of sync for you.

To begin, let's clean your mental slate.

Naturally, you grew up with certain values. You're likely surrounded with other people's values (OPVs). Maybe they come from your work, church, community, or family. Delete their software from your brain, for now. Pretend—if only for the moment—their values aren't yours. If you do this work and discover those OPVs are still a match for you, you're welcome to reload them back into your brain (and no one will be the wiser). But if you don't give yourself permission to expunge them for a minute, you'll keep circling back to where you are now.

Next, scan the list of values on page 48. (Or download it from the toolkit at RedCapeRescue.com if that's easier for you.)

Values

Accomplishment	Friends	Peacefulness
Achievement	Fun	Persistence
Activity	Goodness	Play
Advancement	Helping	Possessions
Adventure	Home	Power
Advocacy	Honesty	Professionalism
Art	Honor	Prosperity
Athletics	Hope	Rebellion
Authenticity	Humility	Recognition
Beauty	Humor	Religion
Belonging	Imagination	Reputation
Career	Improvement	Respect
Caring	Income	Rigor
Challenge	Independence	Risks
Charity	Influence	Satisfaction
Comfort	Inner Harmony	Security
Commitments	Integrity	Self-Expression
Competition	Intimacy	Service
Connection	Joy	Sincerity
Consistency	Knowledge	Social Life
Creativity	Laughter	Spirituality
Culture	Leadership	Sports
Decisiveness	Love	Stability
Discipline	Loyalty	Stamina
Dominance	Maturity	Standards
Duty	Meditation	Status
Education	Modesty	Stimulation
Employment	Money	Success
Enjoyment	Morality	Survival
Entertainment	Neatness	Teamwork
Entrepreneurship	Nonconformity	Tenacity
Equality	Obedience	Tranquility
Excitement	Order	Truthfulness
Exercise	Outdoors	Wealth
Fame	Ownership	Well-Being
Family	Patience	Winning

With clearer values, decisions get easier.

As you scan, circle the ten attributes that feel most like the true and genuine *you*, the heroic version of yourself, the one that's you in your most honest, happiest state. Choose the values you don't want to compromise on. Don't overthink it. I often tell clients to set a timer for no more than seven minutes to help resist censoring or judging their answers during the scan.

If one value on the list isn't quite right but inspires a different word, that's okay, too. If one makes you uncomfortable... also okay. Discomfort is where the growth is.

Once you have your list of ten values, take another two minutes and narrow your list to four—the four that feel most like the hero you aspire to be. Find the four that you wouldn't compromise on, no matter what transpires. If it's hard to narrow them down, then that's another clue about what might be in conflict. Choose your four anyway.

Now... whaddaya gonna do with them?

Good software doesn't work well sitting on your laptop in a zip file. You can't just download it. You have to install it and use it regularly. The list you've just created is your new download. Now, let's run the install in your mental hard drive. That means accepting your values, watching for them, and (the hard part) not judging them. Over time, you'll be able to use them to make better decisions. (We'll talk more about that in the third section of this book, Reinvent What You Do.)

Every value is worthy on its own (value-able, if you will). Sure, I've had clients whose values include learning, teaching, helping. But I've also worked with clients who value beauty, danger, or financial success. There's no right or wrong here. Talk back to your internal judge (use the name you chose in chapter 2 if it helps) and let you be you.

Clarifying your values might take some work. It might make you uncomfortable. But the only way to operate in sync with your values is to first know what the heck they are—all of them. Not what you think they should be. Not what your parents valued. Not what your spouse, boss, or fave Insta celebrity values, either. But what they are, right now, with you just as you are.

You'll not only feel clearer, you'll also feel more confident. You'll make decisions faster and grow more secure about saying yes or no. Then you'll generate the kind of confidence that helps you soar. Give it a try now—you're too valuable to wait.

ACTION PLAN: RESET HOW YOU THINK

Got your top values? Now, answer the questions below.
If you have trouble completing this exercise, answer this
question, too: what's getting in the way? There's no right
or wrong answer, and the few minutes you spend will give
you an operating system for life.

1. How are my collective values showing up in my choices
   right now?

2. Where am I out of sync? Which values am I choosing
   over others?

3. What's working fine?

4. What's the one place I need to take back control and
   match my actions to my values?

————————

Charging to your own rescue,
your defenses are on high
alert. But that's exhausting.
Try this preemptive strategy
to change your mind, fast.

————————

4

IMAGINE POSITIVE INTENT

YOU KNOW that moment. A colleague says or does something that pushes your button. Yep, *that* button. The one that makes your face flush hot, your fists clench, your jaw tighten. Maybe they say *that thing* in an email. You read it, mutter a few choice words to yourself, and start to hammer out a heated response. Your keyboard quietly cries out in pain as you power through the !!!!!s and ????s. You hit send.

Later, after you've sent that blazing email, you discover that the sender meant something entirely different from what you read into it. Your flushed face is now covered in egg.

Prevent this embarrassment. Imagine positive intent.

You might wonder why you have to imagine this. Indeed, why don't we give people the benefit of the doubt, no questions asked? The answer goes back to your big, beautiful brain and all the weird, wonderful things it tries to do to keep you safe.

You'll remember from chapter 2 that your brain is always on the lookout for danger. That's its survival mechanism, honed over years of trying to keep the species alive. For that purpose, it's done a pretty good job.

But for your purposes at work, jumping to conclusions can be a killer.

You see, our brains overemphasize negative experiences and underestimate positive ones. That's why we hear five compliments about our work in our annual review and yet lose sleep over a single item for improvement. Scientists call this the "negativity bias" or "negativity effect." It tricks us into paying more attention to the bad that's happened, rather than instantly seeing the good.

Psychologist David D. Burns describes it this way. Imagine a clear glass of water. Then imagine squeezing a drop of black ink into the glass. Soon, the entire glass turns dark.[10] That's how negative thinking colors our perspective about ourselves and others. But here's the truth: there's still a lot more water in that glass than ink.

Choose the water

What if your interpretation is wrong? What if the other party intended good instead of evil? The decision to choose which thought to believe is fully in your control. That means the next time you get triggered and start to attach a negative meaning to something or someone, you can choose to imagine positive intent instead.

I won't kid you—this mental magic isn't easy, especially in times of change, chaos, and confusion. Naturally, you get worried. People around you are worried. They remind you to fret, even in fleeting moments when you forget that you were troubled. And when you worry, you get wary. Your defenses go up, with metaphorical

What if what you think isn't what they meant?

fists at the ready. Noticing this, you can put your fists down. Lower your walls. See the water, not the ink.

Okay, breathe. That kinda feels good, right?

Positive intent in real life

Alan's ears steamed as he read me the email from his colleague, Carlos. "He's implying I've dropped the ball," Alan vented, "like I haven't delivered my part of the project. I have! And of course, he's copied our boss, the VP, and everyone from my assistant to my grandma."

(For the record, Alan's grandma was not on the cc list.)

His temper was triggered. His fingers itched to fight back, to defend, to prove. As we talked, I challenged him to check his annoyance and, instead, imagine positive intent with the help of a magic question: what else could this mean?

Boom.

The brain is always looking out for danger. But jumping to conclusions can be a killer.

"What else could this mean?" is the pinprick in the balloon of your frustration. It's also the fastest way I know to put a damper on those internal flames so that you can think more clearly.

When Alan asked himself "What else could this mean?" he came up with these potential answers:

- Carlos didn't realize that Alan's part of the project was complete.

- Carlos misunderstood what Alan was delivering and expected something else.

- Carlos was in another conversation with someone cc'd and this note was attempting to answer that person's question.

- Carlos's email was intended to promote himself and had nothing to do with Alan.

- Carlos is just a poor email writer.

- Carlos is an evil warthog and wants to sink Alan's career forever.

When he imagined more positive intent, Alan realized that the most ink-filled scenario, the last item on the list, was likely not true. He also realized he had no way of knowing the truth. That he, Alan, had many stellar talents, but mind reading was not among them.

So he picked up the phone (which, BTW, is often a better way to clarify someone's message than the back-and-forth drama of email or instant messaging). He told

Carlos he'd received his email and said, "I'm wondering if there's something I missed. In your note, it sounded like you were concerned that you hadn't seen my part of the project, but I delivered it to the team on the twenty-fifth. Help me understand—is there something else you needed here?"

As it turned out, Carlos wasn't attacking him at all. He just needed another data point—one that Alan offered up on the spot.

What would have happened if Alan had fired back a blistering email immediately? We don't know. In the experiment of life, there's no control group. But in hindsight, we can guess it wouldn't have solved a darned thing—and could have made things worse.

You're not a doormat, you're a welcome mat

When I teach the concept of imagining positive intent to my fast-track coaching clients, I'm used to getting pushback: "But I know he's trying to make me look bad in front of our boss. I can't just ignore that!" "It's pretty clear that she thinks she could do my job better. I need to stand up for myself."

Now, I'm not suggesting you become roadkill on the superhighway of your career. I'm suggesting you slow down a step, give people the benefit of the doubt, and maybe extend an iota more trust. Imagining positive intent isn't about letting bullies walk all over you. It's not about looking the other way when true offenses take place. It's about interrupting your brain's natural and often destructive pattern, and gathering more information before you respond.

When you do this, you'll welcome new possibilities and see things that you didn't before, such as:

- the pressures the other person might be under, personal or professional

- the moment that came right before or right after the triggering event happened

- the real problem you're wrestling with that you haven't admitted yet (I'll show you how to figure that out in chapter 5)

- a bazillion other things that you might never know, until you step back and ask

Imagining positive intent is proof of your strength and self-control, not your weakness. Sure, it takes a bit of work. Practice. Faith. All things you need to rescue during the inevitable calamities that happen in a long and rich professional life.

Swap frustration for empathy

Have you ever bought an item of clothing online, and once it arrived you realized you'd chosen a size too small? What do you do then? Well, you can keep it and hope your body changes. (Hint: it rarely does.) But rather than squeeze into it or let it dissolve into moth food in your closet, the smart thing to do is to exchange it for something that fits you better.

You can do the exact same thing with the frustration that comes when someone or something infuriates you at work. Send that frustration back to your lizard brain and exchange it for something that fits you better. And that's empathy.

Empathy, or the ability to imagine what someone else might be thinking or feeling, helps us answer the magic question "what else could this mean?" As emotional intelligence expert Daniel Goleman says, "If you can't have empathy and have effective relationships, then no matter how smart you are, you are not going to get very far."[11]

Applying empathy isn't a woo-woo theory. It's a tangible working tool to use every single day. Here are a few examples of the kinds of things you can choose to think with empathy:

- *I heard Michelle's son has been sick. Perhaps she was abrupt with me because she's tired or worried, like I'd be if my son were sick.*

- *David's still new here. I was assuming he knows our processes by now, but maybe he doesn't. It took awhile for me to catch on when I joined the firm.*

- *I know my call caught Terrell as he was headed out the door. He may not have had time to really process what I was asking before he said no. I'll try again.*

When you train your brain to imagine positive intent, you'll see what's happening around you in a new light. Suddenly, you're shining with new possibilities you never would have imagined otherwise.

ACTION PLAN: RESET HOW YOU THINK

Think about the last time your buttons got pushed and you overreacted or assumed the other person meant harm. Hit rewind and put yourself in the moment right before you responded, and answer the following questions:

1. What else could this mean?

2. Why does this bother me? What value is it violating? (Check back with the values you captured in chapter 3.)

3. What am I assuming here?

4. If I trusted this person more, what would I do now?

5. How might I be wrong here?

6. What does the other person need? What do I need?

You're moving away from what's
broken and taking back control of
your life at work. Now, you're ready
to tune in to a deeper source of
direction. So let's learn how to hear
the signals and turn up the volume.

5

LISTEN TO THE WHISPERS

"**W**HAT THE heck was wrong with me?" I kept hearing myself ask, albeit privately, and often while the rest of the world slept.

After all, my life at work looked "good on paper": great company, excellent people, fun projects, generous salary. All of those elements were right, which led me to the conclusion that it must be *me* who was wrong. But at the same time, I heard something else, too—a faint voice inside me, clearly present but as unintelligible as the lyrics of the song playing on the radio down the street.

Back then, I hadn't learned to conquer the battle of the brain (as you did in chapter 2). My bully brain's voice drowned this other voice out, bellowing statements like:

- *You should be happy with what you have.*

- *What right do you have to complain? Plenty of people would kill to work in a place like you do.*

- *You'll never amount to anything more than this, so just stop your damn whining.*

Finally, I got the Cher-in-*Moonstruck* "snap out of it" face slap I needed. It was in that cold McDonald's parking lot I told you about earlier when my beloved boss announced she was retiring and had already selected her replacement—who wasn't me. That jolt amplified the volume of the little voice inside me, and this time, I heard it loud and clear. It said, "*Phew!*"

Yes, much to my surprise, when the next-level-up job was suddenly out of reach (the job that I should have wanted, said the lizard brain), all I felt was relief. That's when I shook hands with the whispers, and we've been friends ever since.

All heroes get messages (but sometimes in code)

In May 2011, TV host–turned-entrepreneur Oprah Winfrey wrapped up her popular, twenty-five-year-old talk show with a lesson.

> Your life is always speaking to you. First in whispers... It's subtle, those whispers. And if you don't pay attention to the whispers, it gets louder and louder. It's like getting thumped upside the head, like my grandmother used to do... [If] you don't pay attention to that, it's like getting a brick upside your head. You don't pay attention to that, the whole brick wall falls down.[12]

Depending on your perspective, you might think of your whispers as "gut feelings" or as "intuition." Do you

My one regret: not acting on those whispers sooner.

answer to a higher power? You may be hearing from your "better angels." No matter what you call them, the whispers are a secret code from your heroic future self, sending you better ways to think about what you need to say and do next.

Your whispers grow up and out from the highest and best part of you: the part that's ready to get out of your current rut and to start feeling happy and strong in your work life again.

Why whisper? Why not shout?

These messages are vital to your long-term well-being, so you'd think that you'd hear them immediately. You'd assume they'd be loud, prominent, and never compromised. But that'd be too easy, right?

Truth is, these secret-not-secret messages usually start small and quiet. They rarely flash across the digital billboard of your daily activities. Maybe that's because our big, beautiful brains crowd them out, trying to keep us from really stretching ourselves, because (gulp) we might fail.

After a while, though, the whispers demand action.

Like Gaby Hinsliff. As political editor of Britain's *Observer*, she enjoyed a powerful career that took her all over the world. But something felt off when she abandoned her seaside vacation, rushing her husband and wailing toddler back to London so she could cover the latest political crisis. Of course, cutting a vacation short never feels quite right, but Hinsliff had felt misgivings before. After all, in the past year, she kept noticing—and dismissing—the small things, like not knowing her son's shoe size or missing weddings, birthdays, and the minutia of her loved ones' lives.

When her husband was offered a job away from hectic London, Hinsliff finally listened to the whispers. In a move that was both criticized and complimented, she left her once-dream job for the life she'd been missing for some time.[13]

Your whispers want attention, too. Like now. If you don't feed them with action, they'll work even harder to be heard . . . only next time, they'll knock you over with a bigger brick (or collapse the wall you've been trying to hold up forever). Yup, you can't ignore the whispers for long.

I'm guessing your whispers led you to think about what's not working in your career, which led you to this book, for which I'm grateful. If so, good for you, because by getting this far, you've signaled to your whispers: message received.

Jan's adventure with the whispers

My client Jan worked in a corporate sales role when she started to hear her whispers.

Like me earlier in my career, she didn't trust those quiet noises. Her whispers were pulling her toward design—a field that, to her logical mind, seemed miles away from what she was doing in sales. After we worked to conquer her battle of the brain (using the strategies from chapter 2), we developed a plan to tune in to those messages from her future self.

First, we got clearer about what Jan's whispers really meant. That way, she could feed them with the right action. After all, the word "design" can mean different work in different situations, but what part of it specifically called to Jan? Sketching out concepts? Searching the world for fabrications? Consulting with clients?

It was time to help the whispers get more specific. When you assume what your whispers mean—or don't mean—without digging deeper into them, it's easy to waste time traveling down the wrong track.

Upon reflection, Jan uncovered that her whispers were pointing her toward working with clients long-term. That was a change from her current world, where she closed a sale and never knew what happened to the client next. With this clarity, we designed bite-sized actions to dig even deeper. Jan chose to:

- identify others in similar roles, scheduling conversations with them to learn more about what their real life was like

- research different roles in her company that consulted with clients

- reconnect with others in her industry through trade groups and LinkedIn

These secret-not-secret messages usually start small and quiet.

Jan's whispers grew louder when she acted. Her actions not only clarified *who* she wanted to be, but also *how* she wanted to be in her life at work. Soon, she could trust the whispers and that her future career would work out.

Don't rebel against the whispers too long

Seven years after leaving my traditional corporate consulting job and starting my coaching business, I was invited to create a decision-making course for career change called "Should You Stay or Go?" As I sketched out lessons, I dug through old files saved from professional development classes I'd taken over the years.

What I found shocked me.

My excavations uncovered a worksheet from a local university's night course, which I didn't remember attending (and still don't). The course was called "Planning for the Future." On that paper, filled out in my almost-illegible, no-I'm-not-a-doctor chicken-scratch, I'd written this:

> I want to make a difference through people—coach professionals through changes, speak to groups all over, and write articles and maybe books on a regular basis.

Reading it, I was gobsmacked. That description is exactly what I do now when I'm doing my most important work. It's exactly what I set out to do when I started my business in 2008. But the shocker?

The worksheet was dated September 2000.

That's a whole eight years before I listened to the whispers that eventually led me to change. And yet my future red-caped self was already calling to me—enough so that I wrote it down.

Suddenly, I understood why people tattoo their bodies with messages of reminder. I, on the other hand, had promptly filed away that vital message from me to me in a battered manila folder, which quickly got buried in the dark recesses of my dusty filing cabinet.

I'll confess: I don't have a lot of regrets in this life, but one thing I do regret is not acting on those whispers sooner. Who knows how many more people I could have helped if I had started my work earlier? Who knows what kind of difference each of those people would be making in their careers and in their lives and, in turn, in our communities and in our world? Thank goodness the whispers kept at it.

Trust the whispers, trust yourself

Once you learn to recognize the whispers, you'll never regret tuning in.

Oh sure, you might wish they'd shut up. It'd be so much easier if they did. But what hero ignores a message for help? What cape-worthy pro hides when it's time to save the day? Not you, I know.

Your whispers will tell you the truth: that somebody out there needs you. Problems in your world of work? They're not being solved on their own. Where are you being called to step in, step up, step out? Where's the pain you're meant to cure, the problems you're meant to solve?

Your hero's whispers never lie. They're trying to tell you the truth that I already know: that we need you to be who you are, doing what you uniquely are meant to do in your career. Trust what the whispers say, and give them a little love and attention. Soon, you'll start soaring again in the new world of your work.

ACTION PLAN: RESET HOW YOU THINK

Let's give your whispers permission to be heard.

1. Plan fifteen minutes of solitude for yourself. Turn off all distractions, including any dings and zings from your phone or computer. (If you need to change your location to have fifteen minutes of uninterrupted time, do that, too.)

2. Take out a sheet of paper (or use the workbook in the downloadable toolkit at RedCapeRescue.com).

3. Set a timer for fifteen minutes, then begin writing with this sentence: *My whispers are telling me...*

   - Write as fast as you're able, and keep writing, even if you repeat yourself. Above all, don't edit, censor, or judge what comes out—there's no right or wrong here. Just give your whispers a safe place to land.

4. When the timer ends, reread what you wrote, ideally out loud.

5. After listening to yourself read what you wrote, answer these questions:

   - How true is this for me?
   - Is the battle of the brain getting in the way?
   - What is one action the whispers are asking of me?

6. If you find you're still struggling with the battle of the brain, reread chapter 2.

Congrats, my dear friend. Reshaping, rethinking, and revising your thoughts is a monumental step in your Red Cape Rescue. It's like grabbing onto an overhead branch and pulling yourself out of the rapids before your dinghy careens over the falls.

It may not feel like much has changed. After all, you're still soaking wet. But you're here, and I'll hand you a towel while we keep sailing toward what's next. In the meantime, remember that you can always go back and review this guide again to:

- revisit what you control
- conquer the battle of the brain
- rethink and reengage with your values
- imagine positive intent
- and remind yourself to always listen to your whispers, the wisdom from the hero inside you

Your life is built on your thoughts. Keep practicing to make these ideas your own.

So, fear not. You've got it. Now, part II will magnify another superpower over which you have complete control: your ability to choose what you say. Go to RedCapeRescue.com to download all of the exercises, plus discover more tools, scripts, videos, and checklists to transform your work and your life. Can't wait to see you there.

REVISE WHAT YOU SAY

Raise your words, not voice.
It is rain that grows flowers, not thunder.

RUMI

———————

Don't be fooled by our soundbite world. Words still matter: both the ones we think and the ones we say out loud. So let's tell a new tale about the hero you're becoming— and the one you already are.

———————

6

REWRITE YOUR STORY

WHEN SOMEONE says, "Let me tell you a story," what do you do? If you're like most of us, you pause, lean in, and prepare to listen. Stories are an essential part of any country, company, or culture, and they're part of you, too.

But wait: the story we're talking about here isn't your so-called elevator pitch. (Don't get me started on how much I despise those: they feel fake and forced, and who wants to talk to strangers in an elevator, anyway?) Nor are we talking about the storytelling that's become a corporate buzzword (and a multi-million-dollar business) in recent years.

We're talking about the story that's the gas in your engine as you drive the highway through change. It's the story that, at its simplest, answers this question: "What do I *say* to others about the road I'm on?"

For you, the "what do I *say*" question may sound something like this:

- "How can I talk about what's not working without seeming like a whiner?"

- "How do I tell my SVP that I deserve this new opportunity without seeming entitled?"

What would happen if a different story was your story?

- "How should I explain that I'm thinking about leaving a well-paying job for what's unknown?"

- "How will I say I got laid off without someone thinking I screwed up?"

- "How can I explain what I want when *I don't know what I want?!*"

In my work with leaders and high-performing professionals, the deceivingly simple question of "what do I *say*?" has waylaid many potential career explorations. As novelist Chimamanda Ngozi Adichie says, "Stories have been used to dispossess and to malign. But stories can also be used to empower and to humanize. Stories can break the dignity of a people. But stories can also repair that broken dignity."[14]

Here's what I know: whether our dignity is broken or merely dinged up, we care about the story we're telling others, and we need the right story in place to motivate and inspire ourselves through change.

A real-world rewrite

Before we work on your story, let's watch how someone else changed theirs.

Maria led a large operations center in her company, serving customers all over the world. She grew up in the organization and was a go-to person for ideas, encouragement, and get-it-done finesse.

One day, Maria arrived at work to the news that her firm had been bought by an organization three times the size. As these things go, with security laws and last-minute deal-making, even as a high-level leader, Maria was blindsided by the announcement. Noting her natural concern, her current CEO took her aside and assured her that the acquisition would create more opportunities for her to grow and be part of the new structure.

The CEO was absolutely right; so right, in fact, that Maria's workload exploded. Suddenly, she was asked to step into rooms full of people she'd never met, talking about things she didn't know.

After a couple of weeks, she called me, exhausted. "I don't understand half of what's being discussed in these meetings," she said. "I'm so afraid of asking a stupid question in front of our new leaders or suggesting something that fails. I'm in over my head here and think it's time for me to look for a new job before I get fired."

After giving her a chance to breathe, I asked, "What if you rewrote that story?"

"Story? It's all true! I'm not making this up!"

"Yup, it's absolutely all true. But what if the story is this: you're so valuable and trusted that no one cares if you're right or wrong; they want to hear your input and the smart questions they expect you'll naturally ask. What if the story is that every single person in the room also feels in over their heads because it's a brand-new experience, and they'd be relieved if someone as honest as you would say, 'This strategy doesn't make sense to me,' or 'Could you explain that financial measure again?' What would happen if *that* was your story?"

For a moment, Maria went quiet. Then, clear-voiced and confident, she said, "That works."

Over the next few weeks, Maria lived her new story and spoke up more frequently. She asked others to explain when what they proposed didn't make sense. She became a role model for her team in being direct rather than trying to impress. Within a year, she was promoted to senior vice president in the new organization. She told me she uses the tool of rewriting her story each time her confidence wanes and she questions her worth.

In Maria's case, both stories were equally true: she was confused and uncertain *and* she was trusted and smart. When you're faced with two potential true stories, why wouldn't you choose the one that helps you, rather than the one that hurts you?

How to shift your story

How do you get from where you are now to the new story that works for you, even if it's not yet happily ever after?

To start, let's shine a light on your existing story. What are you telling yourself and others about your current situation? Write it down, or use a voice memo app on your phone or computer to record it.

Now, read your story out loud, or play it back. Listen for two things: (1) a seemingly powerful outside force and (2) any negative emotions or commentary.

In Maria's example, the powerful outside force was the acquiring company and, more specifically, the leaders she thought she needed to impress. For you, that outside force may be a new boss or colleague, a game-changing technology, or even a family situation that's causing you to rethink your work life.

In Maria's original story, she identified the negative emotions showing up as:

- fear of not being good enough
- confusion about what to do next when she had always known what to do
- embarrassment about not knowing the answers
- and powerlessness

No wonder she thought she needed to leave her job. Throw that old story out. Bury the paper in the backyard if you like symbols and rituals, or drag that sucker's file to the trash on your digital device.

Now, let's write (or speak) a new story: your success story. In this story, give yourself permission to feel clear, confident, courageous. You have total power over all you control (what you think, say, and do). Don't censor or judge your story. Imagine positive (or at least neutral) intent on behalf of that seemingly powerful outside force.

As you did before, write it down, or switch on a voice memo app and hit record.

Maria's revision recognized how much her team needed her. She knew they wanted her to step in and step up with the new leadership. Plus, her story reminded her that she had the broad business acumen to comfortably question new goals and concepts. Finally, she allowed herself to be human and honest, and chose to believe that others wanted to be human and honest, too.

A ground rule as we rewrite your story: it always has to be true.

Funny thing: these characteristics are the ones that have always helped Maria soar in the past.

What's true about you?

The awesome news is that, like Maria, you're free to keep rewriting and strengthening your story as often as you need to. Let's aim to pursue progress, not perfection. And here's one more ground rule as you rewrite your story: it always has to be true.

You're not creating a fantasy world here. You're working with what you've got. But what you've got is likely more than you realize. Think of those Magic Eye pictures you examined as a kid (and maybe still do—hey, no judgment here). On one glance, it's only a bunch of colored dots, but on a second, more careful review (squint, blur, walk away) it's suddenly a vase, a rabbit, or a pool of sharks. Just because you didn't see the sharks at first doesn't mean they weren't there.

Your better story already exists. Right now, you may be too close to it and can't imagine how your "tale of woe" will become a "tale of yo" (groan—sorry). But once you see it and find the right words to say it, then, like the Magic Eye, you won't be able to un-see it. It'll be all sharks, all the time.

If you get stuck, don't give up. Simply begin again. If you keep getting caught in the old story, it might be time to ask for help from an unbiased colleague or professional coach.

No matter how far you are along the path toward what's next, you have changed. You'll never be the same again, and that's just fine. It's time to switch the story you're telling to one that matches who you are now: the you who is soaring once again through your work and life.

That's the best way to find your happily ever after.

ACTION PLAN: REVISE WHAT YOU SAY

Review the "How to shift your story" section and write down or record your own story. After listening to your story and identifying the powerful outside source and negative emotions or brain chatter, dive into these questions:

1. On a scale of 1 to 10, how motivating is that story for you?

2. What's the new story you need to tell—and believe? Write that down or record it, too.

3. If you had a magic wand, what would you love to hear others say about you as they listen to your story?

4. Who needs to hear your new story now? What can you say or do right now to tell your new story to them?

No rescue mission happens singlehandedly. Yours won't, either. Resist the temptation to fly solo and learn this strategy to get the support you need.

7

ASK FOR WHAT YOU NEED

From 1937 to 1952, twice a day, WOR radio in New York City ran a fifteen-minute show called *The Answer Man*. People wrote in (paper letters, given the era) with burning questions like "Who ate the most at the first Thanksgiving?" and "Does a hen lay an egg because she wants to or because she has to?"

Host Albert Mitchell would confidently answer. He had an advantage. Mitchell's office was right across the street from the eminent information source pre-Google: the New York Public Library on 5th Avenue in Manhattan. It's said that he and his staff of forty brainy researchers solved thousands of dilemmas and arguments during their years on the air.[15]

Humans have always asked questions. Today, we're more likely to tap tap tap our Qs into the Googleplex, post our query on social, or even email our fave bloggers or podcasters. So, I think it's false to claim that "people don't like to ask." But it's true that we don't like to ask for things that matter, especially in our lives at work.

We avoid asking for things like:

- a change in expectations or deadlines
- a definitive response or more supportive behavior
- more resources, budget, or team support
- or even a promotion, recognition, updated title, or an increase in salary or bonus

But if we don't ask for what we need, we're missing a crucial component that helps us move forward faster. That magic ingredient is other people.

We love to be asked. Why do we hate to ask?

As a successful super-professional, you make sure everyone else—your clients, customers, colleagues, friends, and family—has what they need at all times. They ask; you answer.

Most of the time, we welcome being asked. When someone else invites our opinion, presence, input, or ideas, we find it hard to resist. We feel needed, useful, wanted. As anyone who's ever longed for a date to the prom could tell you, being asked supports a fundamental human need: to know we're seen and that we're not alone.

So, it's kinda nuts that we like to be asked, but we resist asking, right?

One theory about why this happens is that we mistakenly believe our need for help is crystal clear to other people. Social researchers Thomas Gilovich, Kenneth Savitsky, and Victoria Husted Medvec called this "the illusion of transparency." This is what happens when we believe that our thoughts, feelings, intentions, and needs are oh-so-obvious.[16] I mean, if they were paying more attention, they'd know, wouldn't they?

But smart as we are, most of us aren't wired into the dialogue happening in someone else's mind. (*Oh, you wanted the project update NOW? Why didn't you say so?*)

Here's another theory about why we hate to ask. We worry that the answer might be no. Unconsciously or not, we fret about being rejected; about being seen as incapable, weak, helpless, embarrassed; or about not being good enough. We buy into the classic lawyer's mentality: don't ask a question you don't know the answer to. With all this on top of the complex cultures of our workplaces, it can just seem easier not to ask.

Satisfying, meaningful careers, however, are all about asking. Trust me, you'll get nowhere quickly unless you learn to ask for what you need.

Legendary innovator Steve Jobs knew this. At the age of twelve, Jobs called up electronics innovator and Hewlett-Packard founder Bill Hewlett (whose number, in the day, was listed in the local Palo Alto phone book). When Hewlett answered, Jobs told him he wanted to build a frequency counter (a device used to measure electronic inputs) and wondered if Hewlett had any leftover parts to share.

Hewlett laughed, and not only gave him the parts, but also gave him a job that summer building frequency counters on the H-P assembly line. "I was in heaven," Jobs said.[17]

It's not that we don't like to ask. We just don't like to ask for things that matter.

What might have happened if Jobs never asked? What might the world have missed out on if he waited for others to offer him opportunities instead of asking for his own? What might happen for you if you start asking for what you need today?

How to start asking, now

The most successful asks always involve three foundational steps:

1 Make it personal.
2 Make it specific.
3 Make it done.

(Actually, there's a fourth step that ices the cake: elevate appreciation. It's one of the most forgotten superpowers to tap inside yourself. Since it's so major, we'll talk about it all on its own in chapter 10.)

Step 1: Make it personal

When making the case for a promotion, Gretchen recognized that a change in her role would create stress for her boss, and might generate tension on her team. Her ask wouldn't just affect her own life; it would influence others as well.

That meant she needed to personalize the request. She proposed a plan for how her team would operate should her promotion be granted. "I listed duties that I could easily transition to the team members I had trained," she said. "I outlined how my promotion would be an opportunity for others to grow, and how it wouldn't add work to my boss's day."

Gretchen's preparation didn't result in a promotion at the first meeting with her boss. But after continuing the conversation and anticipating how her advancement would personally affect others, Gretchen was soon promoted to vice president.

Step 2: Make it specific

There's a reason why it rarely works when you ask someone if you can "pick their brain" or "hold an informational interview," especially if you make that ask through email or social media.

Your vague request will get rejected (or, more commonly, ignored) because the person you're asking isn't clear on what you want, and they don't want to be caught off guard facing an ask they're not equipped to answer.

It's another one of those ways our wildly wonderful human brain tries to keep us psychologically safe and protected. Those you want to ask typically won't want to offend or anger you, and they certainly won't want to look stupid or naïve themselves. So it's easier for them to just say no—or to pretend they never saw the email in the first place.

Being specific in your ask allows your answerer to be helpful, faster. Which questions would you find easier to answer?

General questions	Specific questions
Do you know anyone I can talk to about my career opportunities?	Would you introduce me to Angie in your digital marketing department?
Want to hear my idea for an article?	I'd like to write a short article on trends in our business for the trade association website. Who would you suggest I talk to about that?
How do things work in your department?	How are marketing decisions being made?
What's the culture like here?	How does your team typically manage through problems or setbacks?

As social psychologist Heidi Grant notes in her book *Reinforcements*, "Being specific helps the helper to know whether or not they can give you the help you need."[18]

But what if you're willing to make it personal and get specific, but you're still not 100 percent sure of what you're asking, or even what you need? That's to be expected—it's precisely why you need to ask.

When you find yourself unsure of your exact ask, use these phrases to give your answerer a stronger sense of safety:

* "In your opinion…"

* "Based on your experience…"

* "Compared to what you see happening in your company/industry/profession…"

* "From your perspective, what advice do you have on or about…"

Words like these give your helper clear permission to speak from their unique point of view. Now their answer isn't right or wrong; it's merely their opinion. You'll get better, less filtered advice faster.

Step 3: Make it done

In the end, an ask is only helpful if you actually complete it. Yes, you can't control the outcome, but you can control whether or not the ask is checked off your list and not just stuck in your head.

Of course, there are more nuances to asking, such as timing and selecting the right people. You'll find more resources on this topic at RedCapeRescue.com. But let's not overthink it here, 'kay? Asking is a muscle—one you build, like the muscles in your body, through repetition and practice—and it's one of the most important muscles you'll use as you revise what you say.

A specific
ask allows your
answerer to be
helpful, faster.

One more thing:
what if you don't like the answer?

When you're pulling yourself out of a career rut, you might procrastinate your asks. That's usually because you're afraid of what you'll hear. The answers may not be fun, easy, small, or safe.

That's okay. Better to know what others see and think than to be blind to what they know and haven't shared. Knowing is the only way you'll learn, adapt, and grow. But just because something is said doesn't mean it's true.

The best answers often lead to more questions, whether for the same person or for others. Alternatively, you might hear things that, in combination with the other personal and professional development work you're doing, don't make sense for you, at least not right now. It's not unusual to hear wildly conflicting advice from people you know and trust, like "you should quit and start your own business" alongside "starting a business is rough—stay where you are."

Here's the beauty of asking for what you need: you're an adult. You get to accept or ignore the advice, especially if people start telling you your aspirations are off base or you should be "thankful to have a job." Nope. Just because someone sends you guilt, says therapist Lori Gottlieb, "doesn't mean you have to accept delivery."[19] Keep listening to your whispers, just like you learned in chapter 5.

Also, don't base your entire feeling of success on one person's answer. Authors Jack Canfield and Mark

Victor Hansen were rejected 144 times[20] before their classic book *Chicken Soup for the Soul* was published (and went on to become a series of over 250 titles, selling over $2-billion worth of books and related products).[21] Canfield says, "When the world says no, you say next."[22]

"Asking for help is universal," writes Heidi Grant. "The nature of work in the modern world is that you cannot be successful at literally anything without the support of other people. It's the boat we're all in."[23]

Turn your cape into a sail, jump in the boat, and ask. You need others, and we need you.

ACTION PLAN: REVISE WHAT YOU SAY

As you think about where you're headed next, ask yourself:

1. What's one thing you need to ask for now? From whom?

2. What's been getting in the way of asking before now?

3. What homework do you need to do to strengthen your ask?

4. Where do you need to get more specific?

We say all kinds of %*x#ing things when we're under pressure. But a hero uses the power of words for good, not evil. Let's talk about how we're talking, both to others and to ourselves.

8

WATCH YOUR LANGUAGE

WHY DO magicians shout "abracadabra" before they reveal their tricks?

Is it because it's fun to say, a dramatic flourish? Maybe. Is it because it's memorable and repeatable? Perhaps.

But my friend Andy (a dabbler in the art of bunny vanishing) claims the word has true magical powers. He believes that, in ancient times, *abracadabra* evolved from *avra kehdabra*, meaning "I create as I speak."[24]

Well, I can't pull a rabbit out of my hat, but—presto-chango—I can reveal a sleight of hand that will change your life in an instant. Or, more accurately, in this chapter, I'll teach you the sleight of *mouth*.

(That sounds kinda creepy. Sorry. Trust me, it's not.)

Like Andy and his spoon-bending pals, you create as you speak, too. Let me show you how to create more of what you want by using the right words, right now.

When you change your thoughts, you can change your words.

A quick review:
remember your beautiful brain

In part I, you learned this key survival strategy: your thoughts about your current situation are rarely an accurate reflection of the truth. Yes, your brain tells lies (as does mine, as does Amanda Ferber's and Jeff Shank's and Lisa Brzezniak's and everyone else's in this world). It's well intentioned, we know. It's simply using its prehistoric biological programming to keep you safe from harm. Poor little dear.

You can love it for the effort, but at the same time (and in the same breath), you must reject its restrictive messaging that tells you to be afraid, to stay stuck, to worry. After all, if your goal is to stay exactly as you are, then why read this book?

When you recall how your brain triggers your thoughts, you can change your thoughts. And when you can change your thoughts, you can change your words.

Your language = your image

Steve was an aspiring account executive stuck in a copywriter's chair. It was his quick wit and ability to translate ideas to paper that first got him his job as a writer for a local ad agency. Over the years, though, Steve discovered his superpowers were better matched to the client management side of the business, such as selling, persuading, and negotiating.

But no matter who he talked to in his company about this interest, he seemed confined to the same box: copywriter. While there's nothing wrong with being a copywriter, Steve was personally ready for something new. But he believed he had only two choices: find a new job, or stay trapped.

Steve and I met when Acela, a former coaching client of mine, led a team that hired Steve's agency. Acela noticed that Steve was making smart observations about their account and business environment, but she also occasionally heard him say things like, "I'm just a copywriter, so I can't tell you which decision is better," or "You should probably ask the account team." Out of curiosity, she invited him to coffee.

There, she shared her own story. She told him how, as a non-native English speaker joining a U.S. company, she used to talk about herself negatively, with comments like, "Here's the report, but it's not very good," or "I'm not the one you should ask to make that decision." Even though her work was exceptional, each review revealed the same comments: "not ready to be a leader" or "unable to make decisions."

One day, the truth hit her: the feedback she was getting was based on what she was saying. After all, if she wasn't positive about herself, how could she expect others to be? To change the situation, she needed to change what she said.

Acela suggested that Steve reach out to me for help. Through our work together, over time, Steve became more intentional about speaking up with business and client insights. He practiced being more positive and less self-demeaning with his language, saying things like:

- "Based on my experience with similar accounts, I'd recommend..."

- "Looking at the sales data, I see..."

- "As I think about the client's long-term business goals, I think we should focus more on..."

Steve focused on his language over several months, and finally sensed the time was right to pitch a change. He proposed to his leaders that they create a new account position inside the company, one that fit him to a T and filled a hole he saw in the firm's client service model. With Steve's business case in hand (and with his more confident voice at the table), they agreed.

What not to say

In a detailed Stanford University study, researchers tracked hundreds of people trying to meet a wide range of goals, from losing weight to improving their social relationships. They found that the more people criticized themselves, the slower their progress, and the tougher it was to achieve their goal.[25]

As you nobly navigate disruptions in your work and life, falling into the habit of speaking critically is easy, whether you're talking about your situation, your colleagues, or, worse, yourself. In fact, your current colleagues might be unintentionally reinforcing that habit, using dated, fatalistic industrial-age sayings like:

- "Another day, another dollar."
- "You go along to get along."
- "Work is hard; that's why they call it work."
- "Life's a bitch, and then you die."
- "It's not personal; it's just work."

Or you yourself might be saying things out loud like:

- "I don't know what to do."
- "I'm stuck."
- "What's wrong with me?"

Sound familiar? These start as inner conversations (which you know how to handle from your work in chapter 2 on the battle of the brain). Now, it's time to tackle these sabotaging thoughts as they come out of your mouth, too. If these phrases of woe are part of your vocabulary, here's a quick win: STOP IT. If those around you share these moans, STOP LISTENING TO THEM.

(Apologies for the shouting—it's that important.)

Truth is, these Eeyore-esque verbal laments zap your power and energy. If you've been feeling exhausted in your career, I would place a hefty bet that these kinds of words are draining the emotional gas from your tank.

Old-school, negative phrases abound, even in modern workplaces. They imply that you're not in control; that there's some big bad evil entity working against you to offer up another crappy day. But you know that's not

Create more of what you want by using the right words, right now.

true. In fact, you control everything you think, say, and do. So, let's stamp out the useless words and focus on what works instead.

What to say

Comedian Steve Martin said, "Some people have a way with words. Other people... oh, uh, not have way."[26] Maybe you think you don't have a way with words, either. That's okay. The process to say what you need to say doesn't require knowing all the right words.

It requires knowing all the right emotions.

Now, before the PC police start flashing their lights at my use of the word "right," let me clarify: our emotions are never correct or incorrect. They simply are what they are. If you're sad, you have every right to be sad. If you're angry, then damn it, please be angry.

When we speak, though, we become the vocal interpreter of our emotions. Knowing how you feel allows you to more effectively choose what you want to say.

Why? Emotion puts us in motion. When we speak positive words about ourselves (or to and about others), we move forward. When our dialogue is drowning in the negative, those words hold us back, keeping us right where we are or, even worse, digging a hole so deep that climbing out is hard.

At this point in your career transformation, what'd be more helpful to you? Staying in your hole, or building a ladder, rung by rung?

If it's up that you're after, practice speaking words that lean positive, not negative.

Instead of saying...	Try...
I don't know what to do next.	I'm doing the work to figure out what's next for me.
I hate my job.	Parts of my current job are no longer a fit, and I'm working on changing that.
I'm exhausted.	It's time for me to do what I need to do to get some rest, and I'd like your help with that (see chapter 7, "Ask for What You Need").
I don't know what to say.	All I can do is be honest and do my best. I'll figure out the rest from there.
I'm worried about the future.	I'm focused on what I can control right now.

Where your attention goes, words follow

When you're on the brink of something new, inevitably the lizard-brained judge in your head will work overtime to sabotage your thoughts. It's like the new puppy who's peacefully sleeping until the second you're slipping out

If phrases of woe are part of your vocabulary, here's a quick win: STOP IT.

the door, then wham! He's bouncing all over you, leaving dirty paw marks on your pretty party clothes. He means well, but, left uncrated, he'll make you late for hors d'oeuvres.

Thankfully, those thoughts can be changed with more careful attention to the emotions behind them. The same goes for your words.

Words create worlds, and what you say matters. Don't wait for the right words to appear like magic. Create the right ones now to help your ideal situations appear. Watch your language, and abracadabra—your words will lift you up.

ACTION PLAN: REVISE WHAT YOU SAY

Ready to watch your language? Dive into this exercise.

1. Open up a voice memo app on your phone and record yourself talking about where you are in your current career, for about two to three minutes. Just be honest. No one else needs to hear it unless you decide to share it.

2. Now, play back the recording and listen to the words you used. (Some of my clients like to run the recording through transcription software to get a file to print and read.)

3. Write down (or mark) the emotion-packed words that stand out to you.

4. Are your words moving you forward or holding you back?

5. If your words are taking you backward, what are some different words that still feel true to you, but incorporate a more positive emotion? Use the chart in this chapter for help.

6. If your words are moving you forward, great job! What do you need to do to encourage them and help them grow stronger?

———————

Every hero needs a sidekick,

so here's one for you. Say hello

to Discomfort, who's buckled

up beside you as you speed

along your rescue journey.

———————

9

AFFIRM THE SQUIRM

LOOK AROUND you, wherever you are right now. Unless you're wedged into seat 32B or on a gurney in an ambulance, most things around you are built for comfort. Reading in your living room or propped up in bed? Comfort. Hanging out at a local coffee shop or restaurant? Comfort. Listening to this book during a workout? Well, maybe that's not comfortable, but I bet you've chosen your most comfy shoes lest you suffer blisters later.

No wonder we feel like something's off when we move away from what's comfortable, like you're doing right now in your life at work.

A Red Cape Rescue calls you to redefine success—in your job, in your company, in your profession—on your own terms. For most of us, that's just plain uncomfortable. Don't let discomfort stop you, though. It's not a sign that anything's wrong. At this point, you're ready to become comfortable with uncomfortable, and affirm the squirm.

Everybody squirms

I have a weird job. It practically *requires* that I make people uncomfortable, which is something few of us really want to do (although I promise I do it with their best and highest outcomes in mind).

People hire me to challenge, support, and advise them as they build a better work experience, create stronger career prospects, or make more meaningful choices about how they use their time and talents. What I've found is that, no matter what the challenge, there's only one route to those kinds of results, and that's to take the exit to discomfort town.

I know this, study this, teach this. But I'm far from 100 percent immune myself.

Like today. I'm sitting inside on a beautiful sunny Sunday, determined to submit this chapter to my editor, Kendra, by Monday's deadline. I know the weather will chill in a few days, and there's part of me longing to catch as many rays as I can. The overstuffed couch on my back deck beckons, plus I've got a new romance novel waiting for me on my Kindle, promising easy brain candy all afternoon.

Yes ... but no. I committed to the deadline, to completing this chapter, and Kendra's expecting it. Sure, I could weasel some excuse—she knows I'm shoehorning this book into the hours between coaching and speaking and sleeping and living. Or I could tell her the truth—I mean, she lives in *Canada*, for goodness sakes, aka the frozen North, so she knows the importance of honoring a sunny day.

But I *can't* delay. Nope, wrong word. I *won't*.

So, I squirm.

In compromise, I relocate my laptop to the back deck, where, if I squint, I can see my screen and still sit in the sun. It's not optimal; it's full of distractions, like the hawk parked in the tree near me. He's crunching on a breakfast of what appears to be palm rat. I'm fascinated, unwilling to look away, but each minute I allow myself to stare at the hawk as it gnaws rat bones is a minute less in my day to work on this chapter. As he finally flies away, I uncomfortably turn back to my laptop... and squirm some more.

Discomfort is where the growth is

Yes, I'm not immune to the squirm. It ain't easy, doing the things we know we want to do, need to do—the work that matters and makes a difference in our careers and lives.

But here's what I know: discomfort is the only path to growth. There is no substitute.

Take Alison Levine. A world-class mountaineer, she's not only climbed the highest peak on all seven continents but also skied to the North and South Poles. That's despite three heart surgeries and Raynaud's disease, which impacts the circulation in her hands and feet, leaving her at extreme risk for frostbite.

For this adventurer, discomfort—physical and mental—goes with the territory. "The mountains are the ultimate classroom," she said. "These expeditions force you to get to know yourself and to figure out how to perform when you are completely outside of your comfort zone. You learn that you can push yourself far beyond your self-perceived limits."[27]

If you're hungry to break through your limits and climb toward what comes next (and since you're midway through this book, that's a safe bet), you'll learn to override your default settings, which are targeted toward safety and ease. When you do, you'll make room for discomfort's constant presence in your life (and you won't have to freeze your toes off for it, either).

The two faces of discomfort

Of course, like any frenemy, discomfort is two-faced. One side is your buddy, and one is not.

The first face is the discomfort where the work you're doing is truly hard. Maybe you're spelunking for hidden opportunities inside your company or renegotiating the requirements of your job. You're working to create a bigger impact, help others grow, make more meaning through the work you're doing. You care, want to do it right, and something big is at stake. But it's new to you. It's hard.

That's me today, writing to you now. Truth is, I can chat with you individually for hours, dialing in to your specific comfort traps and challenging you to think differently. But faced with stringing together words on a page that are useful, clear, and concise, especially when diving into a monster topic like discomfort... well, I'm kinda struggling.

Make uncomfortable your new comfortable.

But this is *good* discomfort, like at the gym when you increase your bicep curl by five pounds. Your muscles will certainly ache a bit afterward, but you know that means they're growing stronger.

Keep this discomfort around.

The second face of discomfort—the one that's not useful to anyone—is your fear-based pre-programming that kicks in and stops you from pushing that mental muscle to the next level. You know what's happening then, right? Yup, your big, beautiful brain is sending those sneaky messages:

- *You'll never be able to change.*
- *You can't have what you want.*
- *You shouldn't even try.*

Hey, I won't kid you: sometimes it's hard to tell the two faces of discomfort apart. For example, while I'm watching that breakfasting hawk, I'm also watching my thoughts. I notice a few unwelcome ideas, like "you'll never get this book done" and "who's going to read your meanderings, eh?"

While the second face of discomfort often shows up as thoughts, it's the *conversation* you have about discomfort that ultimately makes all the difference. That conversation might be mainly with yourself, but, more often than not, you'll eventually have to talk about your inner hero's aspirations with your:

- spouse or parents
- coworkers or professional colleagues

- boss or leaders
- friends and neighbors
- industry colleagues
- or your chatty neighbor in seat 32A

They might want to know why you're making this next stage of your career so darn hard on yourself, why you can't be happy with things the way they are. Not everyone will understand. That's okay. All you can control is *your* squirm. Others will have to learn for themselves how to deal with theirs.

Speaking up to affirm

The word *affirmation* gets a bad rap. It conjures up visions of naïve secret-seekers repeating hopeful mantras. Personally, I find nothing wrong with a hearty affirmation. (I'll tell you about one I use in chapter 14.) As long as it works for you and is in addition to—not in lieu of—doing the hard work, I say use it.

At its heart, though, an affirmation is simply emotional support or encouragement. When you affirm the squirm, you offer a fortifying nudge away from that sticky feeling—the one that, if left unattended, would have you (or me) lounging in the sun reading Nora Roberts.

(Not that there's anything wrong with that, but that's not today's plan.)

As you commit to making your career work better for your life, you can affirm your squirm when you

Sorry, but discomfort is the only path to growth. There is no substitute.

ask others for their help, advice, or support. Start with phrases like these:

- "I'm not exactly sure how to start here..."

- "This is uncomfortable for me to ask, but..."

- "I'm trying new approaches, and it's awkward, I know."

- "Thanks for listening to what I have to share. It's taken courage for me to put this out there."

- "I've thought about this a lot, and chances are I won't say this perfectly, but I want to tell you about something I'm up to right now..."

- "I'm going to ask for your patience in advance."

- "What I'm going to say might not come out right the first time, so I'll just start, okay?"

Speak to the discomfort. Make the invisible visible for others. It's a heck of a lot easier to see what's real when you shine a little light.

Finally, remember the seed

I once lived in Atlanta, Georgia, and had a small garden in the backyard. I'm more of a weekend hobbyist than a dedicated grower, but I picked up the basics of planting, weeding, and maintenance from kind neighbors and HGTV.

One spring, I decided to indulge my love of sunflowers. I ripped open the package, poured the seeds into my hand, and started daydreaming about the little seeds' journey for the next few months. But the more I thought about it, the less hopeful I felt that by August I'd see blooms.

First, I had to place each seed deep in the hard, spring-cold ground. Then the seed had to break away from its tough shell, stretch out its roots through the packed clay to get nutrients and water, and sprout through the topsoil. Once above ground, the stems and leaves had to thicken, bend toward the light, and (at least in my backyard) fight off hungry squirrels.

No wonder so few seeds make it to flower.

That process cannot be comfortable. If plants made noise, I believe we'd hear them groaning. But that breaking/stretching/pulling/fighting is the only route to growth.

Your heroic self, the one whispering to you, is exactly like those seeds. You may be planted in hard, seemingly unyielding soil. You may be challenged to push your roots deeper to find enough support or to stretch yourself upward to lean into the sun. And just like my sunflowers, you may need to fight off the rascals that will try to stop you, every single day, whether they be scrambling around you or circling inside your head.

Plants can't talk, but you can. Squirming is okay; it's expected. Embrace it and affirm it, out loud and often, in positive and encouraging ways. And whatever you do, keep the squirrels away.

ACTION PLAN: REVISE WHAT YOU SAY

To affirm the squirm, answer these questions:

1. What's the one idea or situation making you uncomfortable right now?

2. Where do you need to affirm the squirm instead of wriggling away from it?

3. Who needs to hear from you about what you're working on or working toward?

4. What do you need to say to affirm the squirm and get the help you need?

When you stumble into the famous dark night of the soul, how do you climb out? Inject positive energy into your words and create a lifeline when you need it most.

10

ACCELERATE APPRECIATION

"HOW DO you find the good when it all feels bad?"

That's the question Mateo asked me.

At forty-six, Mateo was celebrating a great twelve-year career at a tech company in the aviation industry. He had been part of the organization from the early days, starting as one of a few folks around a card table programming code on dueling laptops. Now, he led a team of hundreds all over the world.

One day, though, everything changed.

His company's main client, an airline manufacturer, was forced to ground jets after two fatal accidents. While Mateo's company had no connection to the tragedy, the manufacturer was a primary customer who then shifted its budgets and attention to tackle the crisis at hand—and away from the work Mateo's company was hired to do.

Within a week, Mateo was asked to lay off fifty members of his team, and he himself had been moved to a lesser role in another department.

He was angry. Frustrated. Broken, even, as he described to me at the time.

In each word he spoke, his hopelessness said volumes:

- "How could this happen to me?"
- "I should have seen this coming."
- "I must be getting too old to be in tech."

Each dejected word sent him further into a downward spiral, cementing his belief that his career was done. But it couldn't have been further from the truth.

Appreciation versus gratitude (it's not a competition)

In our initial work together, Mateo and I focused on strategies you've already learned in this book: knowing what you control, conquering the battle of the brain, listening to your whispers, and so on. We revised what he said and reinvented what he did.

But his question about how to find the good when everything felt bad stuck with me and got me thinking harder. Finally, we found a strategy that pushed Mateo out of distress and catalyzed his confidence: accelerating appreciation.

In the past decade, the concept of gratitude has turned trendy, with repeated encouragements to write gratitude journals, meditate on your gifts, and count your blessings during times of crisis. I'm not knocking those strategies; many are scientifically proven, and I often use them myself.

Don't just say
"I appreciate you."
Tell them why.

When you're under tremendous stress ignited by changes at work, though, setting the hurt aside and giving gratitude a little room can be a struggle. You smell fakery, as though you're desperately trying to convince yourself that "I'm happy and whole" when you feel like anything but.

I like to think of gratitude as an emotion, a feeling that emerges in positive experiences, prayers, moments of quiet thanks. Appreciation is the vocal expression of that emotion. It's the emotional punch that makes the gratitude become real, because you've expressed it in a genuine and useful way.

When you accelerate appreciation, you turn your view from inward to outward. You intentionally verbalize more words of thanks. As you do, I promise you, you'll start to notice more things to be thankful for in your life at work, and you'll build the muscle for true, ongoing gratitude that helps you progress.

Appreciation to the rescue

If she was honest, Dany didn't fully respect Saul, the executive director and her boss at the healthcare center where she worked. In her view, he was more focused on paperwork than people, and his communication skills were lacking. Dany had made suggestions in meetings only to have them shot down and her offers to help ignored. So, since on most days their busy paths didn't cross, she only focused on Saul when she had to.

At annual review time, though, Dany was blindsided.

Although her ratings from her peers, team, and clients were exceptional, Saul marked her performance as "below expectations," citing a stubborn attitude and insubordination.

In the same stroke, he asked human resources to place her on a performance improvement plan (or PIP), with a sixty-day "fix it or you're fired" implication.

This was a crappy move by an inexperienced leader. Performance reviews should never be a surprise, and performance improvement plans should only occur after clear conversations about and documentation of performance issues.

But we don't live in a perfect world with perfect leaders, do we? That's how Dany found herself needing to repair the situation, or prepare to leave.

Initially, she considered defaulting to the easy path: avoid Saul altogether and passively play the PIP game with HR (a game almost everyone loses, by the way). She knew that if she did, she'd likely need to start looking for a new job, and other than Saul's leadership, she loved everything about her life at work.

After a little strategizing with me, she chose the alternative: to buoy her courage and schedule a conversation with Saul directly. But how should she handle this conversation? What could she say that didn't feel false but still afforded her an opportunity to see if the situation could be fixed before she gave up?

Dany decided to accelerate appreciation.

At the start of the meeting, she swallowed her pride and took control: "Saul, I just want to start with saying how much I appreciate you sharing your concerns with me. I see how my actions might have looked through your eyes, and I definitely want to hear more to fix it and get us back on the right track. It was never my intention to offend you or seem disrespectful, and I apologize if that's how it felt. I appreciate how difficult it's probably been for you."

Then Dany shut up. She'd prepared in advance for any response: anger, frustration, a tirade outlining all her perceived faults. But her simple words of appreciation worked like magic.

To her surprise, Saul's stance softened. He thanked her for the acknowledgement. He admitted that he may have overreacted and should have talked to her first when he felt frustrated by her behavior. As he relaxed, she became more open, better understanding how their communication got off track, and how she could fix it.

The PIP was torn up within a week. Appreciation saved the day and, probably, Dany's job.

(Quick sidenote: lest you think Dany is the hero here, let's get real. This situation didn't need to get this bad. If Dany had checked her frustration earlier and spoken more words of appreciation about the good things Saul was doing—things she'd noticed but did not focus on—she'd likely have avoided the situation altogether. Lesson learned.)

The three rules of real appreciation

Accelerating appreciation worked for Dany, and it's worked for many of my clients and in my own life. But

Appreciation isn't a magic wand, but it's better than growling at the world.

it's not some party trick you pull out when you desperately need it. Here are three qualities you'll need to hone right away to use this tool now, and always.

Rule 1: Appreciation must be genuine

Even the most clueless humans sniff out fake compliments as easily as they smell bacon sizzling on the stove. And, yes, while some swear that flattery will get you everywhere, Dale Carnegie offered this distinction between appreciation and flattery: "One comes from the heart out; the other from the teeth out."[28]

To use appreciation with Saul, Dany had to dig into her heart and stop gritting her teeth. She used positive intent strategies, like you learned in chapter 4 (asking "what else could this mean?"), to think more deeply about what life must be like from his perspective. Quickly, she saw how complex his daily decisions were. Although she didn't agree with all his choices, she could genuinely appreciate the degree of difficulty in making them.

Rule 2: Appreciation must be specific

Although telling someone "I appreciate you" is better than never speaking up at all, explaining why is always more powerful.

Teach yourself to notice—and call attention to—the positive efforts going on every day. What are all the little things happening that add up to big improvements? What choices, decisions, and actions are taking place all the time that, in the long run, make a big difference? Once you notice these efforts, call them out by saying things like:

- "Hey, Tom, I see that you spent extra time briefing the new hire as we started on our project. I know you're not his manager, but it helped the team, and I'm sure it was helpful to him, too. I just wanted you to know I noticed."

- "Sandra, I wanted to thank you for always bringing a fun, positive attitude to the weekly meeting. The work gets hard sometimes and I notice that you never stop smiling, and I really appreciate it."

- "Jiwan, we may disagree sometimes, but I see how you always have our company's best interest at heart. No matter what our differences, I'm grateful you're supporting us that way."

Your view of someone else may lead them to powerful insights about how they matter.

Rule 3: Appreciation must be offered without expecting a response

In his classic book *Influence*, Robert Cialdini describes reciprocation as "the internal pull to repay what another person has provided us."[29] Unfortunately, many of us have turned this behavioral trick into a ping-pong match: if I say something nice about you, you hit the compliment back to me.

Reciprocating might be a human tendency, but expecting payback is a dead end.

Gone are the days when magazine subscription manager Walter Weintz could mail a letter campaign with two real pennies and gain one million new subscribers in return.[30] (His legendary campaign copy stated: "Keep one penny for bread. Or for luck. Send back the other penny as a down payment on a subscription to the *Reader's Digest*—a penny to seal the bargain!")

Today, only the rare consumer would feel compelled to donate or subscribe because an unknown marketer sent them a penny (or even a dollar or a euro). When a certain response feels expected, not earned, wise professionals tend to resist it further.

In Dany's case, we strategized about what would happen if her appreciation fell on deaf ears, or even if it provoked the lion in Saul that she had seen pop up before. She was prepared to sit, listen, and stay in the mindset of appreciation, taking whatever lumps she needed.

When you accelerate appreciation, you turn your view from inward to outward.

Appreciation isn't a magic wand, but it's better than growling at the world.

Make it specific, not squishy

If the idea of accelerating appreciation still sounds a bit squishy for you hard-nosed careerists, you're not alone. Remember Mateo? He thought so, too.

After all, he'd built his career on horizontal stabilizers, transponders, and RAPCONs, not Oprah-Chopra magical thinking.

With a little practice and a lot of nudging, though, Mateo began speaking specific words of appreciation inside his company to his new and old teams, to his leaders, and to his clients.

He said things like:

- "I see the work you're doing, and it really matters."

- "I know how hard this time has been, and I appreciate how you've stayed on track."

- "Thank you for supporting me right now. I know it hasn't been easy."

Perhaps more importantly, though, he upped the ante by adding more words of appreciation out loud for the person who held the most power over his career: Mateo himself. As author Pema Chödrön says, "It isn't what happens to us that causes us to suffer; it's what we say to ourselves about what happens."[31]

ACTION PLAN: REVISE WHAT YOU SAY

Ready to accelerate appreciation? Start here.

1. What do you need to appreciate within yourself right now? (Can't find anything? How about reading this book or doing these exercises? The things to appreciate are out there—keep looking!)

2. What do you need to appreciate in someone else right now?

3. What do they need to hear? A thank you? A comment like, "I see you struggling and I'm here for you"? Or a "Thanks for seeing me struggle and continuing to encourage me"? Consider this permission to look deeper to find the good.

4. Now, act: send the text, make the phone call, write the Slack message or email. Even old-fashioned snail mail still works wonders.

If I haven't said it already, let me stop and say it now: *Thank you.*

Thank you for reading this far. More importantly, thank you for caring enough about your career and life (and all those in your circle who benefit from both) to pick up this book in the first place. Thank you for having the courage and open-mindedness to try out the simple strategies I've offered here: ones we're rarely taught, like taking back control and conquering the battle of the brain. Thank you for:

- making yourself uncomfortable
- affirming the squirm
- and assuming positive intent, especially when you stumble upon an idea or strategy here that doesn't quite add up for you yet (don't worry; we've got time, and I've got you)

As we march into reinventing what you do, remember we're here for you at RedCapeRescue.com with videos, checklists, scripts, and tools to help you go deeper on all of these ideas so you can apply them to your everyday life. I'll see you there.

PART III

REINVENT WHAT YOU DO

*The most difficult thing is the decision to act;
the rest is merely tenacity.*

AMELIA EARHART

Amid the forest of career change, fear, anxiety, and worry inevitably pop out from behind the trees, challenging you to turn back. Let's anticipate their presence and learn a countermove that'll fend them off every time.

11

FORGE A FEAR STRATEGY

"FEEL THE fear and do it anyway" is useful advice if you're strapped into a bungee at the top of Victoria Falls and the only way out is... down.

In workplace situations, though, when we feel fear, the "do it anyway" part remains significantly optional.

Most "fear" clichés are terrible counsel when we're advancing our careers, yet somehow they're passed along like last year's fruitcake. Truth is, what works in sports doesn't always work at work. With apologies to my friends at Nike, it's usually easier for us to just *not* do it.

But at this point in your career, not doing "it" (whatever that thing is that'll propel you along) won't help. It might even hurt in the long run. There is, however, a solution to any fears you have about the next necessary step to transform your work life, and it doesn't involve phony lines and false platitudes. Let's create a strategy now for when fear hits later.

What is fear, really?

Just to say it, we're not digging into the garden-variety human fears here, like speaking in public or being bitten by spiders. We're talking about the fears that keep you from bringing your superpowers to work: the ones that hold you back from serving the world where you're needed most, and living the life at work that makes you *you*.

In my experience, those fears usually fall into these three categories:

1 *Fear of what others will think:* We're social animals, we humans. We care about the opinions of our inner circle (and often the outer ones, too).

2 *Fear of losing:* In most of our workplaces, we don't fear losing our lives (thank goodness!), but we do fear losing money, status, or freedom.

3 *Fear that we're kidding ourselves:* It's common to refer to this as "imposter syndrome," the feeling of being a fraud. We worry that others will catch on, and we'll be revealed as a fake or phony.

If you've got these fears, congrats: you're normal. As you already learned in part I, fear is your big, beautiful brain's way of signaling you to pause and pay attention.

Paying attention is great. Pausing can be excellent. But when you're managing through work-related change, it's tempting to extend that pause to a full-out stop.

Let's try something else instead.

Your four-letter word to combat fear

Here's a four-letter word you can utter in polite company: *plan*. Having a plan is the secret way to hush up fear and send it to its room. It's how, in the most fear-inducing jobs imaginable, people like Kathleen Clem, an emergency doctor, manage through each day. Kathleen has no clue what illness, accident, or tragedy will roll through her doors at any moment. She stays calm, she says, because she has a plan:

> I first think, "What is the most dangerous thing that this could be? What is the most life-threatening thing this could be?" Only then do I think about what is the most common thing this could be. Most of the rest of medicine looks for a pattern. What does it fit most? And I do that, too, but first I think about what is life-threatening. Because I'm working in an emergency department, and I have to think about that for every patient I see.[32]

Most of us don't work in life-or-death situations. Most of our professional education doesn't teach us how to plan ahead to stave off fear. That's why we need to create our own plans to use as our personal fear-prevention strategy, like my client Anaya did.

When a handful of big players in her industry started purchasing smaller companies like hers, Anaya worried that her company would be next. Consolidation could mean her upper-level job in internal finance would be eliminated. At first, the fear froze her, keeping her up at night. Well-meaning friends tried to talk her out of her fears: "Your company's in good shape," "You have a great job and have nothing to worry about," and so on. Finally, a close colleague suggested she chat with me.

It's never my place, here or anywhere, to talk you out of your fears. They're yours, and Anaya's were hers. But I did ask her, and I'll ask you, too: "If you believe that fear to be true, then what can you *do* about it right now? How can you take control?"

The answers to those questions always lead to a plan.

Anaya's plan focused on people. When the fear kicked up, it signaled her to reach out to someone. Her outreach began as a basic "hello" email or call to an old friend. Soon, she was scheduling conversations with leaders at her own company to raise her profile, communicate her contribution, and assess how others understood her value. Later, she started reaching out to people outside her company every day to build her network and to be more visible in her field.

That plan was uncomplicated but powerful, helping Anaya take back control of what she could do, letting go of the fears of what she would never control.

Start simple

How will you figure out a plan for when fear hits? Let's start simple. Decide on one action that you'll take when you feel the fear, no matter what sparks it.

Your simple plan when the fear hits might be to:

- drink a glass of water
- walk around your desk
- stretch your arms out and breathe for thirty seconds
- wiggle your toes
- dance in place
- close your eyes for thirty seconds
- put on headphones and listen to your favorite song
- ping a friend to ask them how they're doing
- or donate a dollar to a cause you care about

Sound simple, even silly? It's not. It's science.

Actions, even small ones like these, shift our focus and shake up our mental muscle. As author Mel Robbins explains in *The 5-Second Rule*, a small act is a form of *metacognition*, or awareness of your own thought processes. It's a chance to reboot your brain by engaging your body and mind in different ways.[33]

Robbins's strategy is to simply say, "5-4-3-2-1," as if you're a rocket launching. I find that a glass of water and a forward bend are often enough to stop freaking myself out and get back on track.

Play the what-if game

Maybe you've chosen and mastered the one simple action like mine, or like Mel Robbins's, and it shifts you out of fear... for a second.

Decide on one action for when you feel the fear—one small thing, 100 percent in your control.

But right about now, you might be discovering that the ruts your brain has worn into your belief system are hard to climb out of. You keep slipping back into those fears and worries, and they hold you back from doing what you know you need to do. That's when it's time to play a game. Specifically, the what-if game. Or we could call it "Name That Fear." Here's how you play it.

First, write down the fear. Pick the loudest one. Be 100 percent honest; it's just you and me here.

Some examples:

- "I'm afraid I'll be laid off."
- "I'm worried that my boss and I will never get along."
- "I'm concerned that if I take the promotion, I won't be able to handle it."

Now, read that fear back to yourself, and ask, "What if [fill in your fear]?"

- "What if I get laid off?"
- "What if my boss and I never get along?"
- "What if I can't handle the promotion?"

Finally, choose one thing you can do *now* to help plan for that fear:

- "I could be laid off someday. So, right now, I can take a hard look at my expenses and cut back a bit to build up my emergency fund."

- "In case my boss and I never resolve our differences, I can be more deliberate about assuming positive intent and accelerating appreciation with her to improve our communication on my end."

• "In case I can't handle the promotion, I'll review how to ask for what I need [chapter 7] and affirm the squirm [chapter 9] to accept that it'll be uncomfortable as I grow."

When you play the what-if game, you find something to do now to prepare for what might happen later. It gives you a more specific plan, and when you pay attention to the plan, you give less attention to the fear.

Fight the fear upstream

In his book *Upstream*, author Dan Heath recounts a parable about two friends picnicking alongside a river. They hear shouts for help from a drowning child. The friends jump in and save the child, then another comes downriver, then another. Suddenly, one friend notices the other leaving the river before all the children are saved. "Where are you going?" he shouts. The friend replies, "I'm going upstream to get the person throwing all these kids in the water."[34]

Heath explains that this story has often been used by healthcare professionals to question the intensity of effort and investment after a problem has happened rather than anticipating and preventing problems before they occur.

Fear is something you should anticipate. When you're taking new leaps and bounds to change your circumstances at work, you're practically inviting fear, anxiety, and worry to your front door. With a plan based on what you control—what you think, say, and do—you'll tackle the fear in advance and sweep it further out of your way.

ACTION PLAN: REINVENT WHAT YOU DO

Ready to dive deeper? Write down your answers to these questions now:

1. When was the last time you feared something in your career? What did you do?

2. What worked, and what didn't?

3. As you think about your path, what situations spark fear in you right now?

4. What's one small, simple action you can take each time you notice fear popping up?

No matter what the rescue demands, a hero faces choices. How do you decide? How do you pick the right actions and evaluate the consequences? With this strategy, you'll generate fresh alternatives, even when you think you have none.

12

COUNTERACT CHAOS

ARA WAS surprised to find her once-predictable career thrown so off track, so fast.

Less than three months away from a promised promotion, her company unexpectedly sold to a competing firm. But the buyer wasn't merely any competitor: it was her organization's chief rival, the equivalent in her industry of Coke purchasing Pepsi.

Suddenly, the usually confident Lara found herself drowning in chaos. Her team was worried. Her customers were confused. Everything she'd known and trusted at work seemed unpredictable, unstable, and even downright unfair.

Maybe you've been where Lara was. Or maybe someone you love has been trapped in this round room of chaos, repeatedly circling the walls but finding no way out.

Psst: there is a way out.

The only way to counteract chaos is to call on creativity.

What creativity really means

But Darcy, I'm not creative, you might be thinking. To that, I say, "Rubbish." That's a story you're telling yourself (and you have the skills from chapter 6 to rewrite that story). Truth is, all human beings possess a capacity for creation.

Sure, maybe you aren't illustrating children's books, writing haiku, or scripting the next Pixar film, but you're still always creating, adapting, and figuring stuff out:

- School closes for a snow day and you strategize last-minute options for care.

- Your project manager is out sick and you step in to lead the client meeting.

- City transit goes on strike and you rearrange the week so your staff is equipped to work from home for as long as it takes.

And these are only the low-impact incidents. When the stakes are higher, like in the case of an accident, sudden death, or worldwide tragedy, we humans become exceptionally creative, changing our words and ways, sometimes in an instant.

Kate Braestrup knows this to be true. A law enforcement chaplain in the state of Maine, she's a member of the team that knocks on doors to deliver the terrible news of an unexpected death. In holding hundreds of people through that first wave of immense grief, she discovered something remarkable. The initial, devastating reaction never lasts more than half an hour. Certainly, it returns again as people adjust to their loss, but, Braestrup observes, even in the first sixty minutes, people begin creating next steps. They ask, "Where is

To propel yourself out of chaos, make something up.

the body?" "When can we have a funeral?" "What do we do next?" Within an hour, she notes, survivors begin to create their new lives.[35]

When the unexpected happens, whether trivial or tragic, we don't freeze forever. We create what comes next, one step at a time.

We can do that when chaos hits, too.

"It isn't the changes that do you in"

Early in my career, I had the lucky opportunity to study with organizational effectiveness pioneer William Bridges. Bridges created a fresh vocabulary for understanding why creating change in our work and in our lives often fails. He summed it up this way: "It isn't the changes that do you in. It's the transition."[36]

Change itself isn't the problem. In fact, contrary to popular wisdom (and ideas still taught as "change management" today), humans don't resist change. We often initiate it as we move, get married, change jobs, and so on. Change is situational:

- your work moves completely online
- your boss retires
- a new technology is now in place
- and so on

The word *transition* often is used as a synonym for *change*, but the two are different. Transition is psychological: our mind's way through. It's the struggle of closing old doors and bravely walking through new ones, even though we're not sure where they lead.

Bridges popularized a three-phase model for managing transitions in our lives.[37] It's not a brick-by-brick process, but rather a cycle we travel through any time something changes:[38]

1 *Endings:* where you accept what is no longer true in order to move forward.

2 *Neutral Zone:* the temporary wilderness, where you're no longer in the past place and not yet in the future place.

3 *New Beginnings:* your destination, with its clear purpose and direction.

Our friend chaos thrives in that wilderness of the neutral zone, where nothing's certain or clear. It's an anxious, uncomfortable place to be, where it's tempting to complain and do nothing. You want that shining, perfect hero to come soaring in and offer you the perfect role, idea, or solution. Truth is, your hero is always and only you, armed with your unique and natural creativity.

It's all made up

Matt had a plan. He'd been working in his twelve-person law firm for six years, and had been told he was on track to become a partner in another year or two. Managing significant law school loans, Matt decided that those years working toward partnership would allow him to pay off his debt so he could buy a house when he earned partner status.

One day, Matt arrived at the office as the entire staff was gathering in the conference room. The managing partner stood at the head of the cherrywood table and announced that the partners were selling to a large, multinational firm. In six months, the partners—Matt's mentors and advocates—would take buyout packages and retire, and the leadership of the office would change.

Matt went home that night, discouraged that his long-held plan was now on the rocks. Hearing the news, a colleague began emailing Matt job listings, all of which made Matt feel he'd have to leave where he was to start his path to partnership all over again.

Stuck tightly in the chaos, Matt couldn't see a solution. When we met, he said, "I'm a lawyer. I follow the rules. But the rules are changing and I don't know the new ones." It was a classic neutral zone statement: not in the old world, and not yet in the new one.

Matt wanted new rules, so I challenged him to make them up. After all, if no one else is making new rules about the new circumstances, why not you?

To get creative, we used these questions as prompts:

- If this were an adventure movie, what would the hero do next? If it were a drama? A comedy?

- What's the opposite action from what others might expect you to do?

- What would you do if no one cared?

Choose creative action instead of suffering in chaos. It'll always move you forward.

After sorting through a few wild ideas that rocked his buttoned-up sense of what was possible, Matt suddenly discovered a new option.

He realized that his client base and local market knowledge was an asset to the new firm, which acquired the company partly because of its geography. An outside leader wouldn't have that advantage. He also led client relationships that the new organization couldn't afford to lose if Matt moved to another firm.

Rather than remain in wait-and-see mode, Matt took control. He asked the current partners for a direct introduction to their contacts at the new firm and, across a set of meetings, pitched himself as the new office leader.

Matt didn't win the role. But by creatively acting and offering a fresh, innovative solution to a shared problem, he increased his visibility with the new management, showed how he contributes to the firm's success, and earned a retention bonus as the leaders' way of ensuring he didn't leave. Matt's still at the firm, and although he's not yet a partner, he's making more than enough to pay off his student loans.

Say goodbye to chaos

To propel yourself out of the chaotic neutral zone, you'll have to make something up. Step up. Step in. Step out. Your natural (but sometimes sleeping) creative thinking is more important than ever.

Choose creative action instead of suffering in chaos. It's the only way to say goodbye to the neutral zone and hello to the new beginning that you want. Plus, devising your next action is much more rewarding than staying stuck, and a lot more fun, too.

You're ready. Please don't wait. The neutral zone isn't a fun place to be, and too many of us hang out there too long, waiting for a hero to figure it all out. Instead of waiting for a hero, what if that hero is you?

ACTION PLAN: REINVENT WHAT YOU DO

Ready to counteract chaos? Start here, and don't censor or judge yourself based on how you think anyone else would react. If it's something you could do or learn to do, write it down.

1. What's one thing in your career that feels chaotic? Maybe it involves a person, process, or belief.

2. If you could flash to the future and see that one thing changed, how would the change improve your situation right now?

3. Now, get creative. Set a timer for four minutes and write down all the different things you could personally do to reach that future state:

   - If this were an adventure movie, what would the hero do next? If it were a drama? A comedy?
   - What's the opposite action from what others might expect you to do?
   - What would you do if no one cared?

4. Look at your list. What might be simpler than you thought? What's one step you will take now to choose creativity instead of staying stuck in chaos?

As your career resuscitates, your commitments may grow as well. But too many commitments suffocate your future success and distract you from the pursuit at hand. Let's learn the secret to staying on track and thriving in your superpower space.

13

DROP SOME BALLS

'VE GOT a love/hate relationship with the word *productivity*. On one hand, it feels fantastic to get sh*t done and X it off the list. It signals progress, and when you're working hard and moving in a positive direction, progress is worth celebrating.

On the other hand, loading up with a metric ton of to-dos when you're pursuing your dreams is too easy. Everybody has another idea for you: Take that class! Watch those videos! Network with that group! The list of what you *could* be doing is endless, on top what you already *have* to do just to stay where you are.

There's a reason Reinvent What You Do is the last section of this book and not the first. *Do*-ing is a tempting place to start, but you, my fine cape-worthy friend, now know differently. You've learned how to reset what you think, and how those strategies will help you create peace of mind in an instant. You've learned how to revise what you say, so your words make more impact. Finally, you have strategies to rescue what you do.

Those strategies include how to *stop* doing.

Surprise! Yes, there's a success strategy in doing less, without missing out on opportunities, being thought of as lazy, or feeling guilty for not acting like a "team player." Hard for you to imagine? Consider this scenario.

What will you catch?

Pretend you're in a local park, tossing a ball around with a small child. You have a nice, gentle rhythm going, back and forth, back and forth. You're good at this, and it's a fun, rewarding experience.

Suddenly, your mail carrier walks by and pitches another ball your way. Then your boss steps in (where did *she* come from?) and throws another, your neighbor another, your mail carrier one more (his pouch is big, you see).

You quickly field a few and wing them back. It breaks your rhythm and quickens the overall pace, but you keep up—for now. Then the balls start coming faster, and faster, until one smacks you in the head, the child is crying, and your satisfying moment is shattered.

Ouch. If hard, physical orbs were flying at your face from everywhere, you wouldn't dream of trying to catch them all. You'd be forced to let a few bounce.

The same goes for your life at work. Balls = projects, emails, meetings, expectations. You know how many balls you're trying to catch, juggle, and toss back. It's time to decide which balls to drop and which to stop trying to catch in the first place.

You don't have a time problem

These days, the idea of "stop doing things" is almost countercultural. We've been taught that the key to success is to do, do, do, more, more, more. But that, my friends, is a lie, lie, lie.

Celia learned this the hard way. A communications executive for a large global non-profit, she'd built her career with a mindset inherited from her father: when there was more to be done, she would raise her hand to do it. She employed that perspective moving through the ranks, but now, at age thirty-nine with two children and twenty direct reports of her own, the practice of catching all the balls was overwhelming.

"What's wrong with me?" she asked during our first meeting. "Why can't I get everything done?"

Celia's lament is common, I'm afraid. It makes me quietly send a gentle curse to every time-management guru who reinforces the myth that the solution is to "manage your time better."

Celia didn't have a time problem. She had a decision problem.

Celia's decisions looked an awful lot like the ones her dad made. Taking that as a cue, we looked closer at his life. Her father worked his paid profession during a generation when Celia's mother worked full-time in her unpaid profession: managing the home and raising healthy children. Celia's dad also didn't have the blessing/curse of the 24/7 internet and its siren song of accessing information in more places, more often. Her father couldn't have imagined the kind of knowledge-based work Celia now did, executed from anywhere, including the kitchen table.

No, Celia's life didn't look like her father's. Her decisions needed to look different, as well. They needed to look like hers. I'm guessing yours do, too.

"Working hard is important," says Greg McKeown in his book *Essentialism*. "But more effort does not necessarily yield more results. 'Less but better' does."[39]

But how can you possibly transition to less? What's truly *better*?

Smart as we are, you and I are not computers. We're not built to add a new memory chip, replace our motherboard, or upgrade to higher bandwidth. If you're constantly expanding your capacity to catch and handle all the balls coming your way—especially balls that don't make the most of your talents and superpowers—you're draining your resources, not expanding them. That's not helping your company or your career.

Taking on more to the degree that it wears you down or distracts you from what's most important is not a success strategy. It's a recipe for failure. You push your needs into tiny corners of time in between meetings, conference calls, and commutes. Your sleeping habits, healthy eating, or regular walks outdoors can shift to the back burner fast. You end up sacrificing you.

Let's not do that.

There's a success strategy in doing less.

Three ways to drop balls

Okay, you're a bit freaked out at the idea of dropping any of the precious balls you're currently carrying. Although some will bounce and roll, you fear others might shatter into a million shards at your feet. So, let's take this slowly, experimenting with one strategy at a time.

Strategy 1: "Will anyone notice?"

If you just stopped doing it—without saying a word— would anyone notice? Would they care?

For my clients, I estimate that roughly 20 to 30 percent of the balls they decide to drop fall into the "will anyone notice?" category. These include things like:

- reports once needed but whose data is now accessible elsewhere
- lengthy presentations no one needs
- meetings that have lost their relevance or focus
- travel that's been replaced with better remote working and planning tools
- or "nice to have" projects like coordinating team lunches or birthday celebrations

These activities aren't inherently bad or wasteful, but they can quickly become dust catchers of your time, filling your calendar while draining your energy. Often, you can stop these without anyone realizing otherwise.

If someone does notice, try this next strategy.

Strategy 2:"Let's try an experiment"

You're Gerry Generous, and you decide that the weekly department chat you typically attend is no longer a great use of your time. You definitely needed to be there a year ago when the team expanded, but now the team works well and, as you think hard about what's next for you, that meeting no longer feels relevant. You decline the weekly meeting invite to see if anyone notices (strategy 1).

Then you hear from Tom Timesucker, your peer who runs the meeting.

Tom says, "Gerry, why aren't you coming to the department meeting? You know it's important."

That's when you start a new conversation with Tom and propose an experiment:

> Tom, right now, it seems like the team's working well and I don't think you need me for an hour every week. Instead, I think the team would benefit more if I focused that time on [name another team priority]. So, for the next month, I'm going to try an experiment. Starting on [date 1] and ending on [date 2], I'll stay out of the meeting. It may work; it may not! But no matter what happens, I expect this experiment will give all of us other ideas about how to make our work easier and still get the results we want. Of course, I'm here if the team has questions, and on [date 2], I'll check back in with you for input on whether my presence has been missed.

Now, if Tom Timesucker is in a position of power— say, a boss or client—and you're worried they'll be offended or hurt by your experiment, you might decide

> # When you catch all the balls, colleagues can't tell that something has to change.

not to drop a meeting and explain later. Instead, you'll want to try the final strategy.

Strategy 3: "Here's an alternative"

Pitching an alternative is similar to trying an experiment. But in this strategy, you'll propose a specific swap that reduces the burden on you or makes the task at hand more productive or fun.

Say something like this:

> I know we're all looking for ways to create more time in our days so we get more of what matters done. I had an idea. For the next month, instead of [the activity you'd like to change], we could try [describe your proposed activity]. If it doesn't work, we can always go back to what we were doing, but if it does, I think it will be useful for all of us. Are you game?

Don't think you have alternatives? Here are a few ideas to get you started:

Instead of...	Try this alternative...
Taking meeting notes	Record the conversation and post the audio file and/or transcript
Creating a complicated PowerPoint	Create a one-page summary with the key findings
Holding status meetings	Ask each team member to answer the same two or three questions on video by the same deadline each week, posted in a common place (Slack, Google Drive, or other internal cloud location)
Letting meetings run long	Keep a timer visible to create a sense of urgency

Fair warning, though. When we're longing to revisit an obligation or task, most of us default to this third strategy first. Don't. Tend to the low hanging fruit with the first strategy before you start involving others. Resist the urge to ask for permission. Asking "is this okay?" traps us back into the thing we most wanted to eliminate. When you start by seeing whether anyone notices the things you're dropping, you'll be surprised how much you'll clean from your plate without anyone the wiser.

Dropping balls is good for your company

If you can't imagine that your leaders, colleagues, clients, or customers will accept your decisions, look closer at how they benefit, too.

When you catch all the balls, you become a sponge, sucking up all the excess that's floating around. For others in your company, your sponginess obscures the fact that it's time to hire, eliminate outdated processes, change a role, or reward your contributions. In the long term, that's unhealthy for the company, your department, and your team.

Your willingness to take it all on also makes it harder for your customers or colleagues to appreciate your full value. Managing expectations becomes more difficult, since you've protected them from how much work happens behind the scenes that they never knew about (or paid for).

Plus, when you catch all the balls, colleagues don't know that anything's amiss. They can't see that you need support, or that a process or expectation needs to change. They can't read your mind and often create their own story about why you take on so much:

- "She's a workaholic."
- "He doesn't know how to say no."
- "They always do it this way; they'll never change."
- "He's too detail-oriented and doesn't know that 80 percent done will be good enough."
- "She's just slow with her work."

Since you've sponged up all the visible mess, with no balls sitting there untouched, no one else notices which problems need to be solved. No one realizes what your true worth is. After all, everything's handled—but at a cost only to you.

Do your company a service while saving yourself. Drop some balls today—then hold tight to the few that matter most.

ACTION PLAN: REINVENT WHAT YOU DO

Time to drop some balls? Start here.

1. Set a timer for four minutes.

2. Write down every work-related task you spent time on during the past week. Don't censor, rank, or judge. Just squeeze everything out of your brain as fast as possible.

3. Now, which of the tasks on your list do you dread or procrastinate? Which are outside the superpower space where you're at your best and highest use? Put a check next to those items.

4. Of all the items you've checked, which, in your wildest dreams, would you eliminate right now? What would happen if you stopped doing it? Who would notice? What would they do or say? Use one of the strategies in this chapter to start dropping that ball.

Look at you—you've soared to new heights. Amazing. So how do you make sure you'll never need saving again? Grab the tools to keep your hard work working for you.

14

MAGNIFY MOMENTUM

LUCILLE BALL'S first drama teacher wrote a letter to her parents, saying, "She's too shy and reticent to put her best foot forward."

By the time of her death more than sixty years later, the comedienne had earned four Emmys, induction into the Television Hall of Fame, and recognition for her life's work from the Kennedy Center for the Performing Arts. Ball had also become the first woman to run a major Hollywood studio, not only producing shows starring herself and her then-husband Desi Arnaz, but launching the original *Star Trek* and *Mission Impossible* series, too.[40]

What if Lucy had taken that initial criticism to heart? What if she'd listened to well-meaning family and friends and decided to become a shopkeeper instead?

The world would have missed out on Vitameatavegamin, plus the funniest assembly line of all times. (If you're not sure what I mean, go look up these classic *I Love Lucy* episodes and thank me later.)

Lucy didn't simply have guts, chutzpah, or talent. She knew how to make things happen for herself.

A body in motion

At this point, you have the tools in hand to repair whatever was broken in your career:

- You know how to reset how you think.

- You can revise what you say.

- You're reinventing what you do (and, as you learned in the previous chapter, what you can drop to make more room for what you want to do).

Superstar, you've come so far. Now, how will you keep moving forward, no matter what happens? How will you resist the inevitable comments from naysayers that tell you "you can't" or "you won't" or "you shouldn't"? How do you avoid the workplace habits that tempt you to stay small and stuck or to forget all the new ideas you've learned here?

There are two items you need to magnify your momentum and keep your foot on the gas.

Item 1: Your success structure

Allow me to illustrate the importance of a success structure with an example from my own backyard. One year, I tried to grow tomatoes. Wandering my local garden center that spring, surrounded by seedlings from across the veggie universe, the idea seemed so tempting. I loaded up a few tomato plants, hauled them home, plopped them in a big pot, and trusted them do their magic.

Contrary to popular belief, structure is your friend.

I watched in delight for a few months as they sprouted. Each plant sent out tiny yellow flowers that miraculously turned into green ovals, precursors of the final fruit.

That's when I made my mistake.

If you've ever tried to grow a tomato, you know you can't just plant it and leave it alone. The eventual tomato is heavier than its branches will hold. You need a stake or cage to give the new growth more security, something to hang onto during its precarious journey upward. You need to provide structure that will support what the plant's growing into, not what it was at the start.

It's the same with me and you, my little tomato. For our momentum to grow properly, we need a success structure to support us.

Too often, we think of structure as a restriction or limit. We balk at complex organizational frameworks that are supposed to clarify decision-making but instead complicate the process.

You can't grow in the status quo.

In this case, though, structure is your friend. Success structures allow you to set up your environment in a way that helps prop up your desired future.

A structure might mean involving others who'll hold you to your desired path:

- "I've given Angela permission to call me out if I start criticizing myself or my work."

- "I'm investing in a career coach to keep me on track when these changes I'm making get hard and I'm tempted to give up."

- "I asked my wife to text me a little love note a few times a week, reminding me of the bigger goals I'm working on in my career and in our lives."

Alternatively, your success structure might be environmental or physical. For example, if you work from home, packing your files and tech into a briefcase or box at the end of the day may provide structure to separate work from family time. Or, as author James Clear says, you can "habit stack" a new structure on top of one already in place, such as, "After I pour my cup of coffee each morning, I will meditate for one minute."[41]

No matter what your structures look like, creating systems to support your refreshed direction will ensure whatever's blooming inside you won't rot in the dirt.

Item 2: Your momentum mantra

It's hard to grow in the status quo. Going forward, you'll need an essence of energy, a spike of stick-to-it-iveness, and the faith of forgiveness when you mess up. That's why, in addition to your success structure, the second tool you'll need is a momentum mantra.

Your momentum mantra is a phrase, statement, or even memory to turn to every time you get stuck or feel like you're losing your way.

Call it an affirmation if you want. A repetitive statement simply functions to remind the mind about where we want it to focus. It's an auto-tuner for your channel-flipping brain, returning your thoughts to the station where you want to place your attention.

Your momentum mantra needs to reflect the new you, the one wearing your red cape. It's a statement of the identity you'll claim going forward, even if you're not completely there yet.

Momentum mantras in motion

Jackson rescued his career when he recognized how much precious family time he wasted suffering the "Sunday blues," anticipating to-dos ahead at work. After doing the exercises in this book, Jackson realized that, in the guise of being a "team player," he'd been too quiet about where he was spending his time and that his company needed more of his higher-value work. Over time, he renegotiated his job responsibilities and elevated the mix of his day-to-day work. His momentum mantra became "I stay true to my superpower space, at work and at home."

Erin's momentum mantra became "I'm someone who doesn't criticize what I can't control." She'd received tough 360 feedback from her peers calling her hyper-critical and claiming they could never be good enough to meet her standards. The comments crushed Erin, who genuinely thought of herself as helpful, not hurtful. As we looked deeper at her actions, we noticed her habit of jumping into conversations and replying to emails with an implicit criticism about everything. Nothing and nobody seemed good enough or made the right decisions in her eyes. Her mantra reminded her to change her mind.

Alan, who learned to control his hair-trigger response to the email from Carlos in chapter 4, decided to check his quick-judging tendencies with the momentum mantra "I don't jump to anger; I imagine positive intent first."

What's yours? It might sound something like these:

- "I'm a person who makes time to listen to the whispers and act on them."

- "I ask for what I need, always."

- "Remember that time I faced that hard decision? I handled it fine, and will handle what comes."

- "I don't let work get in the way of my workout."

- "I have a 100 percent success rate of making it through my worst days."

- "I always make the best decisions I can with what I know at the time."

A momentum mantra tells the mind where you want it to focus.

Mine is "Somebody out there needs me." You're welcome to borrow it if you like, because it's true for you, too. Yes, I forget this from time to time, especially in those moments when the phone isn't ringing or a client's struggling with the counsel I'm sharing. When those things happen, though, somehow I always stumble back across my mantra. It reminds me of where I'm headed and why.

Losing momentum happens. I promise it'll happen to you (although that's a sucky promise to make). But when it does, you'll know what to do. Return to your success structure, and use it. Speak your momentum mantra, and believe it. As Lucille Ball said, "I get my spontaneous performances out of knowing exactly what I'm supposed to do."[42]

You now know what to do. Oh, and for how long? As long as it takes to bounce back on the path toward the hero you need to be now. You've got this—keep the momentum going.

ACTION PLAN: REINVENT WHAT YOU DO

Ready to magnify your momentum? Start here:

1. What might get in the way of your progress? List everything that springs to mind, no matter how small, odd, or unlikely. It all counts.

2. Review your list. What one or two items are most likely to happen?

3. With those items in mind, what's the success structure you need to combat them and maintain momentum?

   - Who can you ask for help? What do you want them to do?
   - What can you put in place in your environment or physical space?

4. What momentum mantra will you turn to when you get stuck?

   - What phrases, sayings, or stories inspire you?
   - Where will you use it now?

———————

If we only claimed victory when everything was ideal, we'd never celebrate at all. That'd be a shame, because you've come so far. Let's learn how to honor the work you've been doing, even if the road to recovery still seems long.

———————

15

PURSUE PROGRESS

I F LIFE was like InstaFaceTube (or whatever the hot social site is when you read this), we'd all be thin, well lit, and happy.

But here's my warning: the quest for perfection is a false path. I know, you've heard this before from a kazillion magazine articles. But they're often the same mags that airbrush the heck out of a gorgeous model's face, and so we struggle to really believe that it's okay not to be perfect.

Let's try a different route, and pursue something other than perfection. Let's pursue progress.

The truth about perfection

The things you do will never be perfect. *Eeek!* Sorry. That's hard for most of us to internalize. But better to learn it now than to struggle forever.

Jason Parker knows that kind of struggle.

At age three, he enrolled in his first skating class. At age twelve, he'd won a championship and was on the fast track toward his dream: the Olympic Games.

Jason trained six to eight hours a day, six days a week, for eleven months out of the year, for fourteen out of the twenty years of his career. But no matter how hard he trained his body, he came short of making the Olympic team: not once, not twice, but three times. With four years between each main event, that translates to missing his dream for twelve years. As he tells it:

> I can remember I was supposed to pack my bag, I was supposed to actually go to another training camp in Mont Tremblant, Quebec. And I came to this point. I full-on broke down. I broke down in tears, out of exhaustion. And I started to wonder, I started to actually think, *You know what, I don't think I can do this anymore.*

Jason was ready to give up. For his tired, bruised body, perfection seemed out of reach. Then, as he tells it, his girlfriend (later his wife) walked in, noticed his unpacked bag, and, for the first time, watched this world-class athlete cry. He remembers her words:

> You know what, Jason? I support you 100 percent. You're right, you have had an amazing career, you have done far more than you thought, far more than anybody thought you ever would. So the one thing I want you to think about is, Will you ever look back at the end of your life? Will you ever look back and wonder, *What if?*

That, Jason shared later, flipped a switch.[43] If he didn't act—as in, pack his bag and catch his flight—he wouldn't arrive at the next camp. If he didn't do that, he couldn't make the next team. If he didn't make the next team, he would never compete at the Olympics. *Of course* he would wonder "what if"!

All he needed was progress, not perfection. He needed to stay in motion, taking the next small step, doing the next logical thing. When he looked at it like that, progress became possible.

The high-performing professionals I work with are a lot like Jason (albeit without the hamstrings of steel). They pressure themselves to get it right: for their projects to work, their teams to be terrific, their ideas to take off. They want everything they touch to progress without a hitch. It's probably what you want, too.

But life, especially life at work, doesn't happen like that. When you measure your success in terms of perfection, you feel frustrated and overwhelmed. You always come up short. But it doesn't have to be that way.

BTW, Jason packed his bag that day and, in 2006, won the Olympic silver medal in team speed skating.

The science behind progress

Yes, sometimes there's a medal, a promotion, a handshake, a magazine cover. But for most of us, those so-called celebratory moments of our life at work would fill a shot glass. We need better tools to quench our thirst to know we're on track.

As Harvard researchers Teresa Amabile and Steven Kramer found, that tool is progress. Amabile and Kramer didn't set out to understand progress. They

It's time for more TA-DAs.

were interested in discovering what managers do to drive creativity—and what behaviors kill it in our modern workplace. As part of their research, they recruited people from twenty-six project teams within seven companies. At the end of each workday, the researchers emailed their study participants with a few short questions about how the day had gone, and asked them to hit reply with answers. Teams participated between nine and thirty-eight weeks, with an average of nineteen weeks. In the end, this yielded 11,637 daily questionnaires and diary entries.[44]

The researchers found (and subsequently reported in *The Progress Principle*) that the single most important factor influencing how positively the participants felt about their work was whether they progressed on something meaningful to them, even if that progress was small.

Progress, it seemed, is the true measure of whether someone feels successful in what Amabile and Kramer call people's "inner work life." Done, they discovered, is better than perfect.

The challenge the researchers found, though, was that most of us can't always identify when we've made progress. In our work environments, projects take years to complete, with hundreds of hands touching them in addition to ours. It's harder and harder to know when to celebrate our contributions and to honor our progress.

Therefore, I believe it's time for more TA-DAS.

Find your TA-DA

In 2012, I was lucky enough to travel to China with my dad. Although we marveled at the Great Wall, the Terracotta Warriors, and the fresh-made dumplings (oh, the dumplings!), one of my favorite lessons arrived during an acrobatics performance in Shanghai.

Now, this show had "tourist trap" written all over it. After a long day of walking the crowded, hot streets of the city, though, we were ready for a cool night of entertainment. And what entertainment! Bouncy boys soaring through the air, catching each other with both strength and grace. Clever women balancing dish after dish atop their heads. Plate spinners, gleefully running back and forth across the stage in a careful frenzy, keeping everything in motion.

But what has stuck with me most are the TA-DAS.

You've seen a TA-DA. It's that move where we toss up our arms in a celebratory V, throw back our shoulders and pause, for a moment, basking in the energy of what we've just accomplished.

TA-DA!

When we say it out loud, we lovingly lengthen the last syllable, squeezing the most out of the *ahhhhhh*.

TA-DAS are typically the sole province of Olympians, circus folk, and toddlers proudly waddling, arms up, toward their parents. Right now, I bet you can even hear the two chords that often accompany the move: *TA-DA!*

It's the more enthusiastic, less fancy cousin to the French *voilà*. (It's also the opposite of the sad, comedic *womp-womp*.) It's an onomatopoeia, a word that sounds like the original sound it's meant to evoke. Although there's no precise record, *ta-da* seems to have originated in the early 1900s, when an orchestra leader encouraged his musicians to end with a flourish—the kind of long and short notes that let you know the king is about to appear. He said, "Let's hear a ta-da," and the rest is history.[45]

In the cool, dark theater of my Shanghai show, I'm guessing we witnessed about twenty TA-DAS, presented by each of the performers with equal enthusiasm and met with a healthy round of applause and appreciation.

But here's the fascinating thing.

Not every performance was perfect. Sometimes, the acrobats fell, spectacularly. Once in a while, a plate shattered. Still, no matter the outcome of the trick, at the conclusion of the act, each performer struck a bold TA-DA. I invite you to do the same.

You deserve more TA-DAS

Where are your TA-DAS? I challenge you to look closely at the work you do each day—work you've been adapting and adjusting along the route of your Red Cape Rescue:

- That difficult conversation you had with your boss? TA-DA!

- The decision to drop a ball and let go of a commitment that no longer matters to you? TA-DA!

- Intentionally accelerating appreciation in a meeting that is not going well? TA-DA!

- Catching yourself thinking you're not good enough and immediately correcting your mental language? TA-DA!

- Making your way to the end of this book? TA-DA!

You get the idea. You, and me, and plate-spinner Zhang Wei all deserve to honor our progress: our committed, diligent, day-to-day work, no matter if it crashes or not. When we let go of the pressure valve of perfection, we see the TA-DAs in every new thought, word, and action we take in our newly transformed world of work.

It's time. Throw your shoulders back, shake out your red cape, and raise those hands in the air. You've more than earned the applause.

ACTION PLAN: REINVENT WHAT YOU DO

Pursue progress, not perfection, as you answer these questions:

1. Where are you waiting for things to be perfect? What would perfect look like?

2. What would progress look like on your biggest effort today? Where is the TA-DA?

3. How will you start noticing your progress each day?

4. Who could help you see your progress more clearly?

You're almost at the end of this book (TA-DA!). Good for you. I'm honored. If you've done the work along the way in each chapter's Action Plan section, even better. That alone puts you way ahead of the pack.

If you haven't yet gone deeper into the questions, no worries. They're not going anywhere. And if you'd rather have them all in one place, remember you can visit me at RedCapeRescue.com for these plus more supporting tools.

By traveling this far, you've proven you've got what it takes to navigate whatever's next in your career. Give yourself a pat on the back—not everyone's brave enough to walk this path. In fact, for every incredible person like you, there's a handful of others nearby with the same depth of possibility, with the same raw talent and heart—but they're stuck and don't know what to do next. You know the feeling, right?

If you know someone like that, now's the time to do them a favor. Teach them one of these ideas. They'll appreciate you for it. I know for a fact that these strategies save careers, which might also save families, communities, and lives. You may be the hero someone is waiting for. So, before you go, a few final words to make sure your Red Cape Rescue sticks.

CONCLUSION
NOW, KEEP YOUR CAPE ON

T HE NAME Disney is synonymous with happiness, but it wasn't always that way for the creative genius behind the name.

Walt Disney was derailed over and over. His first cartoon company went bankrupt. In a contract dispute, he lost the rights to his first successful cartoon character, Oswald the Lucky Rabbit. (Mickey came later, and who remembers Oswald now?) Broke and despondent, Disney suffered a nervous breakdown.

By the time he died in 1966, more than 240 million people had seen a Disney film, 80 million had read a Disney book, and 100 million had watched a Disney TV show.[46] Biographer Neal Gabler explained that Disney, the son of a cold and abusive father, had persisted against great odds to create a fantasy world for himself in which he would feel loved and safe. Disney ended up spreading that feeling to the world.[47]

Life's funny like this. There's no control group. We can't run an A/B test and know what Alternative Walt

Disney would have done had his father been kind or if he'd never experienced pain or failure. We only know what *was* done.

Same goes for you as you make choices in your career right now. You want to make the best decisions you can, mapping out all possible angles. But you can't know the what-might-bes. Since you can't predict the future, how can you maintain perspective? How do you continue to stay in control of what you think, say, and do? How might you direct your mindset, create your own stories, and creatively act to not just survive, but thrive in your life at work?

The secret is to choose happiness

Seriously, happiness?

Yes, happiness gets a bad rap in our cynical workplaces. Despite the acres of detailed research in the world of positive psychology, many of us still cringe at the thought of our work making us "happy."

We're comfortable seeking to be engaged in a mission or important effort. We're okay talking about "workplace satisfaction," as if it's a single measure across multiple humans. But happy? We're surprisingly still uncomfortable with thinking and talking about that.

You may even wonder if happy is even possible in today's gripey, chaotic life at work. Well, I say yes. Down deep, I believe you know it is, too.

You're the only person tasked with making you happy in your career and life, together in harmony at

You don't need to pretend you're a hero. You already are.

the same time. Making yourself happy is the real job you take on during your Red Cape Rescue. As author Shawn Achor says, "Happiness is the joy you feel moving toward your potential."[48]

As you experiment with the techniques in this book, I offer you permission (if you choose to accept it) to use what makes you happy as your compass, your true north. Feeling good is good. Keep conquering the battle of the brain, and allow yourself to pay honest attention to the whispers telling you what's making you feel that joy, that happiness, that uplift that keeps your cape waving behind you.

Truth is, your emotions are the most powerful lever of all as you create change in your career. Positive emotions like happiness, joy, and—dare I say it?—love, even at work, elevate you above it all, no matter what happens that's out of your control.

Surprised? You're not alone

Most of us have been taught there's no room for emotion at work. We were told "It's not personal, it's just business" or "There's no crying in [fill in your dry-eyed industry here]."

Well, we've been taught wrong.

Work is always personal. It's deeply human to want to care about our contributions, to understand and see how we matter. As living, breathing beings, we're uniquely equipped with emotions, and it's a mistake to think we shouldn't bring them to our lives at work.

In fact, emotion puts us in motion. Positive emotions like happiness propel us forward. Negative emotions hold us back. As you test out each of the fifteen strategies in this guide, my big wish for you is that they infuse you with more positive energy every single day. Maybe you experience hope or encouragement, a sense of progress or possibility, or the simple, reassuring feeling of accomplishment that you took action rather than waiting for the world to change.

You don't need to pretend you're a hero. You are one, red cape and all. In fact, you're the hero you've been waiting for. Please don't doubt it, hide, or play small, because we need you to soar, now more than ever.

GRATITUDE

AS YOU read in chapter 10, I'm a huge fan of accelerating appreciation. In fact, my biggest fear is that the words on this page won't show enough gratitude for all the hard-working professionals and inspirational souls who made this book come to life.

But I'll try.

First, huge hugs to every single one of my Insiders at RedCapeRevolution.com. Some of you have been reading and responding to my weekly notes for years; others may have just found me yesterday, but you all matter greatly. In fact, if it wasn't for a response from Arvida in Seattle, I may never have written this book. Thanks also to the subset of those Insiders who decided to follow my behind-the-scenes journey in getting this work into the world. Your enthusiasm and support matters more than you know.

My private clients over the years have invested not only their money and time in me but also something significantly more valuable: their trust. For that, I'm forever grateful. In the interest of continued confidentiality, you're not named here, but I hope you see your stories and successes in these pages and toast yourself once more for the hard work done.

I'm grateful to Pam Fultz, Melinda Lee, and Lauren Redding for promoting the pandemic-inspired audio series that eventually led to what is inside this book. Shay Ben-Dov and Cheli Brown both took early stabs at adapting my spoken words to the page, and both taught me something about what I was trying to say but hadn't crystalized yet. Thank you.

My first Zoom with Jesse Finkelstein left me soaring, and I was excited and a bit intimidated to work with her top-notch publishing team at Page Two. Prior to our kickoff, they asked me to write out my big vision for this book. I wrote my desired future: that the global pandemic of 2020–2021 would be in our rearview and I'd get to celebrate this book with many of you live, all over the world. I trust that's come true (and if it hasn't, just remember: I'm not virtual, I'm real).

As a long-time blogger who has worked hard to find my own voice over the years, I tend to write how I speak: sometimes rambling, sometimes abrupt for dramatic emphasis. My editor, Kendra Ward, accepted the challenging task of balancing my quirky voice with quietly fierce advocacy for you, my reader, the most important person in this entire equation. The book's hugely better for her presence (plus, there's a thirty-page document of "leftovers" that'll make for adequate blog fodder someday soon).

Much thanks to my small-but-mighty Red Cape team of Deb Pelham and Lei Ann Finch, and the rest of the not-so-small but oh-so-mighty Page Two team, including Trena White, Peter Cocking, Megan O'Neill, Melissa Edwards, and Rony Ganon, plus the aforementioned Jesse and Kendra. The brilliant and kind Marci Bailey added her research chops and journalistic skill, and helped me practice asking for what I needed. Jennifer Kahnweiler, Rebecca Whitecotton, Kristina Paider, Leslie Ehm, Mo Bunnell, Melissa Montuori, Colette Auclair, Jennifer Trammell, and Chrissi Jackson are among the many who went out of their way to offer special help and encouragement, and I'm grateful to them all.

Hank, my sweet neph-dog, I'm sorry to exploit your sweet face a few times too often in my emails, but my Insiders love you as I do, too. I owe you a BarkBox.

Dana and Cookie, thanks for keeping me in charcuterie and wine, with a healthy side dish of support and love. Dad, we miss you. I'm guessing there's an excellent library where you are, or why would they call it heaven? Maybe you'll be able to read this there.

Finally, but never final, I'm grateful for the love, patience, and encouragement of my mom, Joyce Eikenberg, for knowing that typing = working and for understanding how I can stare out the window and never notice it's dirty. I love you and am so honored to be your daughter.

NOTES

1   David McClelland as quoted in Raj Raghunathan, "Why Losing Control Can Make You Happier," *Greater Good Magazine*, September 28, 2016, greatergood.berkeley.edu/ article/item/why_losing_control_make_you_happier.

2   Seth Godin, *Linchpin: Are You Indispensable?* (Portfolio, 2010).

3   John A. Shedd, *Salt from My Attic* (Mosher Press, 1928).

4   Ethan Kross, *Chatter: The Voice in Our Head, Why It Matters and How to Harness It* (Crown, 2020).

5   Penn Medicine, "Fight or Flight: The Science of Fear... and Why We Like Scary Movies," October 2, 2017, pennmedicine .org/updates/blogs/health-and-wellness/2017/october/fear; Harvard Health Publishing, "Understanding the Stress Response," updated July 6, 2020, health.harvard.edu/staying -healthy/understanding-the-stress-response.

6   Shirzad Chamine, *Positive Intelligence: Why Only 20% of Teams and Individuals Achieve Their True Potential and How You Can Achieve Yours* (Greenleaf Book Group Press, 2012).

7   Patrick A. Coleman, "Felicity Huffman's Parenting Site 'What the Flicka?' Showed a Real-Life Scary Mommy," *Fatherly*, April 4, 2019, fatherly.com/love-money/felicity-huffman -what-the-flicka-mom-publication-scary-mommy; Kate Taylor, "Felicity Huffman and 13 Others to Plead Guilty in College Admissions Scandal," *New York Times*, April 8, 2019, nytimes .com/2019/04/08/us/felicity-huffman-guilty.html.

8 Mark Manson, "Personal Values: How to Know Who You Really Are," MarkManson.net, accessed April 19, 2021, markmanson.net/personal-values; AppSumo, "How to Create a Healthy Value System: Mark Manson," YouTube, June 9, 2020, youtube.com/watch?v=Jb6B5HilQM4.

9 Brant Menswar, *Black Sheep: Unleash the Extraordinary, Awe-Inspiring, Undiscovered You* (Page Two, 2020).

10 David D. Burns, *Feeling Good: The New Mood Therapy* (William Morrow and Company, 1980).

11 Daniel Goleman, *Emotional Intelligence: Why It Can Matter More Than IQ* (Bantam Dell, 1995).

12 Oprah Winfrey, *The Oprah Winfrey Show*, May 25, 2011, oprah.com/oprahshow/the-oprah-winfrey-show-finale_1/8.

13 Gaby Hinsliff, "I Had It All, But I Didn't Have a Life," *The Guardian*, November 1, 2009, theguardian.com/culture/2009/nov/01/gaby-hinsliff-quits-working-motherhood.

14 Chimamanda Ngozi Adichie, "The Danger of a Single Story," TEDGlobal, July 2009, ted.com/talks/chimamanda_ngozi_adichie_the_danger_of_a_single_story.

15 Albert Mitchell, "Thanksgiving Questions," *The Answer Man*, via OldTimeRadioDownloads.com, first aired November 23, 1944, oldtimeradiodownloads.com/gossip/the-answer-man/thanksgiving-questions-1944-11-23.

16 Thomas Gilovich, Kenneth Savitsky, and Victoria Husted Medvec, "The Illusion of Transparency: Biased Assessments of Others' Ability to Read One's Emotional States," *Journal of Personality and Social Psychology* 75(2), April 1998: 332–46, psycnet.apa.org/record/1998-10511-003.

17 Silicon Valley Historical Association, "Steve Jobs on Failure," YouTube, October 31, 2011, youtube.com/watch?v=zkTf0LmD qKI&list=RDCMUCMIUCjJ3Ca84cf3iA1P9UhQ.

18 Heidi Grant, *Reinforcements: How to Get People to Help You* (Harvard Business Review Press, 2018).

19 Lori Gottlieb, *Maybe You Should Talk to Someone: A Therapist, Her Therapist, and Our Lives Revealed* (Houghton Mifflin Harcourt, 2019).

20 All About Book Publishing, "Truth About Publishing," January 2021, allaboutbookpublishing.com/7590/truth-about -publishing.

21 Chicken Soup for the Soul, "Facts & Figures," accessed April 13, 2021, chickensoup.com/about/facts-and-figures.

22 Jack Canfield, "How to Reject Rejection," JackCanfield.com, accessed April 13, 2021, jackcanfield.com/blog/how-to-reject -rejection.

23 Grant, *Reinforcements*.

24 World Wide Words, "abracadabra," accessed March 19, 2021, worldwidewords.org/qa/qa-abr1.htm.

25 Michelle McQuaid, "3 Ways to Turn Self-Criticism into Self-Compassion," *Psychology Today*, April 26, 2016, psychology today.com/us/blog/functioning-flourishing/201604/3-ways -turn-self-criticism-self-compassion.

26 Steve Martin, "Philosophy/Religion/College/Language" (vocal performance), *A Wild and Crazy Guy* (Warner Bros., 1978).

27 Alison Levine, quoted in Mandy Antoniacci, "3 Key Lessons from Climbing Mount Everest That Challenge Our Views of Success," *Inc.*, April 18, 2016, inc.com/mandy-antoniacci/ critical-lessons-from-climbing-mount-everest-that-are -refining-leadership.html.

28 Dale Carnegie, *How to Win Friends and Influence People* (Pocket Books, 1936, 1998).

29 Robert Cialdini, *Influence: The Psychology of Persuasion* (Harper Business, 1984, 2006).

30 Edwin McDowell, "Walter H. Weintz, 81, Pioneer in Direct Mail," *New York Times*, December 25, 1996, nytimes.com/ 1996/12/25/nyregion/walter-h-weintz-81-pioneer-in-direct -mail.html.

31 Pema Chödrön, *When Things Fall Apart: Heart Advice for Difficult Times* (Shambhala Publications, 1997, 2016).

32 AMA, "What It's Like to Specialize in Emergency Medicine: Shadowing Dr. Clem," AMA-assn.org, August 8, 2017, ama -assn.org/residents-students/specialty-profiles/what-it-s -specialize-emergency-medicine-shadowing-dr-clem.

33 Mel Robbins, *The 5-Second Rule: Transform Your Life, Work, and Confidence with Everyday Courage* (Savio Republic, 2017).

34 Dan Heath, *Upstream: The Quest to Solve Problems Before They Happen* (Avid Reader Press, 2020).

35 Kate Braestrup, *Here If You Need Me: A True Story* (Little, Brown and Company, 2007).

36 William Bridges with Susan Bridges, *Managing Transitions: Making the Most of Change*, 25th anniversary edition (De Capo Lifelong Books, 1991, 2017).

37 Bridges, *Managing Transitions*; Association for Talent Development, "Obituary: Transition Pioneer William Bridges," accessed March 19, 2021, td.org/newsletters/atd-links/obituary-transition-pioneer-william-bridges.

38 William Bridges Associates, "Bridges Transition Model," accessed April 13, 2021, wmbridges.com/about/what-is-transition.

39 Greg McKeown, *Essentialism: The Disciplined Pursuit of Less* (Crown, 2014).

40 Biography.com, "Lucille Ball," updated March 2, 2020, biography.com/actor/lucille-ball.

41 James Clear, "How to Build New Habits by Taking Advantage of Old Ones," JamesClear.com, accessed March 21, 2021, jamesclear.com/habit-stacking.

42 Amanda Harding, "Lucille Ball Almost Broke Her Nose Filming 'The Candy Factory' Episode," *Showbiz Cheat Sheet*, September 24, 2020, cheatsheet.com/entertainment/i-love-lucy-lucille-ball-almost-broke-her-nose-filming-the-candy-factory-episode.html.

43 Jason Parker, email to author (used with personal permission), May 2021, JasonParker.co.

44 Teresa Amabile and Steven Kramer, *The Progress Principle: Using Small Wins to Ignite Joy, Engagement, and Creativity at Work* (Harvard Business Review Press, 2011).

45 Dictionary.com, "ta-da," accessed March 19, 2021, dictionary.com/browse/ta-da.

46 Paul Harris, "The Cruel Reality of Disney's World," *The Guardian*, November 26, 2006, theguardian.com/world/ 2006/nov/26/film.usa; Eudie Pak, "Walt Disney's Rocky Road to Success," Biography.com, updated June 17, 2020, biography.com/news/walt-disney-failures.

47 Harris, "Cruel Reality."

48 Sean Achor, "The Happy Secret to Better Work," TEDx-Bloomington, May 2011, ted.com/talks/shawn_achor_the _happy_secret_to_better_work.

ABOUT
DARCY EIKENBERG, PCC

LIKE MANY of us in the working world today, Darcy Eikenberg wears a lot of hats. She's been an executive coach to leaders at organizations such as The Coca-Cola Company, Microsoft, State Farm, Deloitte Consulting, and more. She consults and speaks about career growth, employee engagement, and leadership development all over the world. She blogs regularly on leadership and career issues at RedCapeRevolution.com. Her ideas have been shared in the *Harvard Business Review*, Thrive Global, CNN.com, The Ladders, *The Atlanta Journal-Constitution*, and *Forbes*, among others. She's a former principal and communication consulting business leader at Hewitt Associates, now part of Alight Solutions, and she graduated from Northwestern University. Darcy brings a sense of humor to serious matters in our work and careers, and she offers simple, practical ways we can transform our lives at work, right where we are, right now.

FIND MORE RESOURCES AT
REDCAPERESCUE.COM

If you're ready to go deeper into your Red Cape Rescue, we're here to help. As promised, we've organized more tools, scripts, and videos for you at RedCapeRescue.com. Stop by and download a complete workbook of the exercises that appear at the end of each chapter, or click to find the latest ideas for your real-life rescue, no matter what's happening for you in your career. You'll also be able to invite me to speak at your next event (and I'd love to see you!), get bulk copies of this book for your team, work directly with me, or participate in an on-demand course or live workshop (online or in-person).

Plus, when you sign up (free), we get to keep in touch on a more regular basis, to stay relevant on what's happening in the real world of work. I love hearing your stories and I learn from every one of you, every day. Go to RedCapeRescue.com now and I'll see you there.

CPSIA information can be obtained
at www.ICGtesting.com
Printed in the USA
LVHW021140170921
698064LV00003B/8